SEDONA - SACRED EARTH

SEDONA - SACRED EARTH

ANCIENT LORE, MODERN MYTHS
A GUIDE TO THE RED ROCK COUNTRY

by Nicholas R. Mann

Published by **ZIVAH** Publishers, Prescott, AZ

Many thanks to:

Vera Louise Drysdale, Taira, Max Licher, Rahelio, Naomi and White Bear, Antoine
Seronde, Terry Walsh, Dee Morris, Page Bryant, Ross and Arthur. A special thanks
to Nancy Dye and Margaret Thompson for their invaluable editing and adventurousness,
to Carol Horn for bringing the players together, to Adele Seronde for her heart,
and to Anne Williams for the music that inspired the understanding of the harmonious
composition of the landscape of Sedona making this book possible.

Frontispiece, *Bell Rock Temple*, and illustration, *Komwidapokuwia Emerging*,
on Page 11 by Vera Louise Drysdale.
Photo on Page 35 by Margaret Thompson.

We gratefully acknowledge Harcourt Brace Jovanovich, Inc. for permission to quote from *Four Quartets*
by T.S. Eliot. Thanks also to Robert Bly for the quotation from *News of the Universe* on Page 78.

Maps, Photos and Drawings by Nicholas R. Mann unless otherwise accredited.
Sedona - Sacred Earth © 1989 and © 1991 Nicholas R. Mann.
Bell Rock Temple and *Komwidapokuwia Emerging* 1990 Vera Louise Drysdale.
Chant on Page 82 © 1989 Anne Williams.

First Printing, March 1989
Second Printing, July 1989
Expanded Edition, January 1991
13 12 11 10 9 8 7 6 5 4 3 2

Published by ZIVAH Publishers, 545 Ellenwood Drive, Prescott, AZ 86303.
Printed by Classic Printers, Prescott, AZ.

ISBN 0-9622707-3-3
LCC 90-71401

Front cover, Bell Rock.
Facing page: Contemporary medicine wheel, hand pictograph and Long Canyon cliff dwellings.

Table of Contents

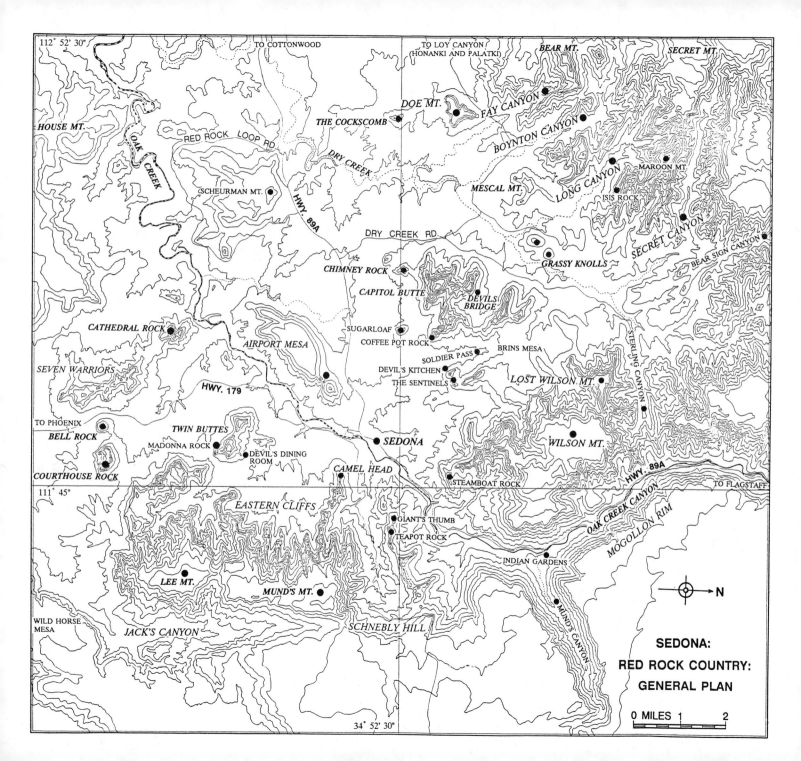

SEDONA:

RED ROCK COUNTRY:

GENERAL PLAN

0 MILES 1 2

Introduction

When a friend suggested that I write a book about Sedona, my initial reaction was that it would take years to get to know the area well enough. As an outsider, and British at that, the idea seemed impossible. Time went by, and so did the hikes, and I came to realize that although I could not pretend to be an expert on Sedona, I could write a book on what I did know about - geomancy or the study of earth energies - and apply that purely as an exercise to the Sedona landscape.

The aim of this book then, is to give examples of geomantic applications to the Sedona landscape. It is not for me to say that "this is how it is," but rather to allow the readers, through familiarizing themselves with the concepts of geomancy, to apply those concepts for themselves, and in doing so come up with their own interpretations, based perhaps on a deeper local knowledge than my own.

I was trained in the European Geomantic Tradition. Most of my knowledge comes from Britain, Ireland and Scotland. It is primarily based on experience of sites dating to the megalithic period. At that time there was an awareness of the land as a living entity, and a worldview which brought together practical and religious elements to enhance the well-being of all life. The building of structures such as stone circles, stone rows, chambered mounds and the placing of standing stones in complex, often geometrical patterns, appears to have been carried out with a specific and visionary purpose in mind.

These practices re-appeared in the medieval period, especially in the great cathedrals which were constructed according to geometrical principles based upon the universal canons of proportion. At this time ideas from other esoteric traditions were introduced into the Western world, such as energy centers or chakras within the body, and their application to the landscape or the temple.

The art of geomancy has always been an integral part of architecture and landscape design in China. There, the practice of Feng-Shui aimed for the achievement of terrestrial harmony through the balancing of the elements of the natural landscape. This was done according to principles which allowed the fusion of the White Tiger and the Blue Dragon, or Yin and Yang energies, to take place.

Throughout this book, in addition to attempting to define basic geomantic principles, I have given examples of their application to the Red Rock Country surrounding Sedona. The examples drawn from the megalithic period are primarily the ley lines; from medieval practice, the construction of geometrical landscape temples; and from Chinese Feng-Shui, the analysis of the forms of hills and mountains. I have also collected what few available Native American traditions relating to Sedona I could find; and, as a result of this exercise I have drawn the various strands together in the final chapters and have given a suggested form for what I would call The Sedona Landscape Temple.

I offer it to you in the spirit with which it was revealed to me. I hope it is useful for the greater understanding and unfoldment of the potential of what is indubitably a sacred landscape, and that it may be a source of further and greater inspiration for all who come here.

Nicholas Mann

Nicholas R. Mann - January 1991.

Looking southeast toward Wilson Mountain and Sedona from Brins Mesa.

Chapter 1

THE RED EARTH

These rocks have weathered into fantastic shapes suggestive of cathedrals, Greek temples and sharp steeples of churches extending like giant needles into the sky.   J.W. Fewkes. 1895.

The Making of a Story

The mysteries of Arizona's Red Rock Country lie deep within the earth. The millions of years of geological formation - deposition, faulting and erosion - tell of a history of earth changes which has left a landscape among the most beautiful and spectacular in the world. Anyone who has made the journey from Flagstaff down Oak Creek Canyon when the autumn colors are at their peak and has taken a moment to look at the subtle reflections in the river and the towering crags above knows that this place holds the power and the magnificence that lifetime memories are woven of.

The successive waves of settlers: the prehistoric peoples, then the Hohokam and the Sinagua - the ancestors of the contemporary Indians - then the Yavapai, the Tonto Apache, the Spanish, the first white pioneers and finally the latter day settlers, visitors and spiritual seekers have all left their mark on the landscape and have made their contribution to Sedona's singular story. Their dreams, aspirations and fears, coupled with their technological and material abilities, have determined the physical impression they have left behind on the nature of the land. As this impression has

been slight up to the modern day, it seems Sedona's story is still in the making. That which is being made today and that which is still to come, is and will have an impact upon the natural landscape greater than anything from the past.

In this sense Sedona is a new landscape, not an old one. Sedona's story is being made now and will be made in the future. The landscape is responding to the thoughts, actions and the myths laid down by modern people - even the names are modern, not ancient as in the rest of the world. And so it could be said that what Sedona is lies in the future in interaction with the geological past. Its full meaning is yet to come.

On the other hand, although there has been a radical discontinuity from the native cultures and they have left little to make a physical impression, the landscape has been deeply imprinted by the telling of legend. For at least among the native peoples of historical times, Sedona was held to be a sacred place. It was a place of emergence, of regeneration and of connection with the spirit world. It is these traditions that the first part of this book intends to explore, and it is these traditions that contribute to the sense of sanctity that draws many people to Sedona today.

The Red Earth

Red, the color of the Sedona earth, figures strongly in many ancient native traditions. Among the Hopi many of the clans include Palatkwapi - the Red City of the South - in the legends of their migrations. The place of the red earth was a great cultural and religious center before its destruction by flood at the end of one world cycle. Many Native Americans also speak of the Good Red Road, the path of return to the world of Spirit.

It has been said by Jade Wah'oo, a traditional shaman of Mongolian and Native American lineage that among the Mongolian peoples the final home of the goddess Sedna, the goddess of balance and harmony, is where the "Castle of Red Rocks bears her name." In Australia, Uluru, the huge red sandstone formation in the central desert is the emergence point and resting place of many of the world-creating ancestors. And among the European traditions there are legends and songs which tell of the life-giving, sacred powers associated with the red earth.

Red ochre, a naturally occurring mineral substance, is used among tribal peoples all over the world in religious and ritualistic ceremony for body painting. It signifies the life-force for the Australian Aborigines. It is easy to see how red ochre corresponds to fire and to blood. In Europe, although it is not known what the exact significance of red ochre was for all of its various peoples, it has been found in many prehistoric tombs and was used extensively for wall painting in deep caverns. The red hand appeared frequently, as it does in the pictographs of the Southwest and we still find it being used among the Aborigines.

In research among isolated tribal peoples, anthropologists found that "red" was the primal and sometimes the only color for which a name existed. Things were either "black" or "white," the terms for which were not strictly translatable as colors. What was neither black nor white was "red." These colors frequently form a triad of a sacred nature for prehistoric peoples and remain so today for those whose native traditions have been maintained.

In Chinese, and indeed in the mainstream of the European Tradition, red corresponds to the South, to Mars, to fire, to summer, and in its aspects of Feng-Shui, to pointed hills such as Bell Rock. Allegorically it refers to the "Red Bird," the Phoenix, the mysterious bird which went through fire to renew itself from the ashes. The word "Phoenix" has its origin in the Greek and Phoenician term for blood.

The Historical Background

For many years it was the resort of hostile Apaches, who fled to its recesses where they were in comparative safety. A few renegades yet seek its vastnesses as a secure hiding place from their pursuers. This basin is as yet almost wholly unknown, except to the military, who from time to time have pursued the Indians into its wonderful canyons and gorges.
Hiram Hodge - 1877.

A piece of information often heard by the visitor is that Sedona was a sacred place to the Indians, so sacred that they did not live there. What proof is there for this?

From what little is known it seems that Indians were not in permanent residence in the Canyon Country at the time the first settlers arrived. This is hardly surprising given the policies of the Americans from 1870 onward to induce the Yavapai and Apache to settle on reservations. In the winter of 1875 about 1,400 Yavapai were made to walk from the

Verde Valley Reservation to the San Carlos Apache Reservation. 100 died on this "March of Tears."

Back in Oak Creek in 1876 the first settler, J.J. Thompson, found gardens abandoned by the Indians and brought them back to life. The military view of the settlement, now known as Indian Gardens, was that it was a temporary one made by "renegade Apaches." The military and the settlers in Arizona at the time did not wish to distinguish between the Apache and the peaceable Yavapai as they wanted to claim the land and the water rights for themselves.

It was, however, a branch of the Yavapai calling themselves Wipukpa who lived in the Red Rock Country. "Wipuk" was their name for Sedona and means "at the foot of the rocks or mountains." The gardens in Oak Creek Canyon were most likely planted by them. Before examining the Yavapai traditions in more detail though, let us see what can be learned from still earlier times.

The Spanish explorer Antonio de Espejo followed the old trail from the Hopi mesas to the mines in the Verde Valley in 1583. He encountered Indians as he came down off the Colorado Plateau through Rattlesnake Canyon and Dry Beaver Creek, just to the south of Sedona. The Indians were Yavapai who pursued a nomadic lifestyle utilizing the resources of a wide area. As Espejo or the Spanish who came after him never went further north, nor were they really interested in the people, we have no idea from them how the Indians viewed what is now Sedona.

The archaeological evidence reveals that the Verde Valley up to and including the Mogollon Rim was extensively occupied by the people known as Sinagua in the period roughly between 500 and 1400. These people settled alongside the rivers and reveal traits resembling the Hohokam who lived further south in what is now the Phoenix area. After the eruption of Sunset Crater in 1050 they also settled on good farmland east of Flagstaff to the north, where they were influenced by the Anasazi. Between 900 and 1300 large pueblos were being built in the region, for example, Tuzigoot, Montezuma Castle, Wupatki, Sacred Mountain and Clear Creek Ruin. These formed a part of the development of the sophisticated pueblo culture that was flowering throughout Mesoamerica.

In the Sedona area, dwellings were constructed at this time in recesses along the canyon walls and on the summits of the mesas. The heaviest concentrations of habitation were in the canyons surrounding Dry Creek. Ruins can be seen north of Gray Mountain, on Doe and Mescal Mountains, in Secret, Long, Boynton, Hartwell and Fay Canyons, beside Oak Creek at House Mountain and to the west in Red (Palatki) and Loy (Honanki) Canyons. Rock art can be seen in all the canyons. It is probable that a trail passed through Sterling Canyon and descended into Oak Creek Canyon, indicating that the site of Indian Gardens may have been utilized at this time.

The first archaeologist to investigate the area, Jesse Walter Fewkes, wrote in 1895 that "in the well-wooded valley of Oak Creek...(there is) evidence of aboriginal occupancy on all sides - ruins of buildings, fortified hilltops, pictographs and irrigating ditches - testifying that there was at one time a considerable population in this valley. There is scarcely a single canyon into these red cliffs in which evidence of former human habitations are not found in the form of ruins."

Further evidence from the Dry Creek area shows that a quarry site had been in use there by still earlier peoples. Tools and other charred remains found near the road crossing gave an approximate age of 4,000 years and were probably far older. Stone points found in Sycamore Canyon were likely to be 10,000 years old. Apart from evidence of settlement we have no clues as to how Sedona figured in the worldview of the ancient people.

Other ruins have been found on Steamboat Rock, in Woods Canyon, above Red Rock Crossing, on Courthouse Rock, on Wild Horse Mesa where a settlement has a ball court showing Hohokam influence and to the south in the Beaver Creek area. These show that the Sinagua extensively occupied the area around Sedona until their "disappearance" from the whole region by 1400.

The period of migration which followed has led to much speculation. A multitude of causes for the migration has been suggested, from plague, to war, to overspecialization and dependence upon canal systems, to drought. There is much confusion but this much is clear; people do not in normal circumstances "disappear" but cultural styles do alter. Absorption and assimilation of new technologies, new world views and new strategies in subsistence can lead to the disappearance of one cultural style and the appearance of another among the same people.

The Hohokam - "those who have vanished" - and the Sinagua - "without water" - were the ancestors of later peoples who may have migrated northward along the Palatkwapi Trail to become a part of the Hopi culture. Others followed the rivers south to form part of the cultures of the Yavapai, the Pima and Apache. It was these people who were settled in the region by the time the Spanish explorers arrived. But we have little insight into how these people viewed Sedona except for pieces of tantalizing evidence from the Hopi and the later legends of the Yavapai.

The Palatkwapi Trail running from the Hopi Mesas to the mines around Jerome and Prescott is the oldest and most used trail in the region. Later on known as the Chavez Trail

SEDONA	VERDE VALLEY	SOUTHWEST
8000 Archaic period. Nomadic Hunters.		
2000 Points found in Dry Creek. Meso-American influences.		
B.C.		
A.D.		
500 Pit Houses along Mogollon Rim. Agriculture develops.		
Colonization of Verde Valley by Sinagua.		
Migrations -	Hohokam influence from South.	
	Mogollon influence from East.	
	Anasazi influence from North.	
800 Population increases.	----	Extensive trade.
900 First Pueblos and Kivas.		Anasazi predominance.
1050 Eruption of Sunset Crater.		Chaco Canyon.
Widespread commerce.	----	Great Pueblos.
1100 Pueblos more common. Montezuma Castle.		
Tuzigoot.		
1250 Honanki and Palatki.		Chaco declines.
1275 Period of drought everywhere.		Mesa Verde abandoned.
Clear Creek Ruin, Tuzigoot,		
Sacred Mountain, etc. at peak.		
1300 "Forts" on uplands.		
1325	Pueblos in decline.	
1400 Pueblos abandoned throughout whole area.		
Migrations.		Pueblos on Hopi Mesa,
		Rio Grande, Zuni, etc.
Apache - Navajo enter area.		
1500 Yavapai - Tonto Apache. Nomadic hunters.		
1583	Arrival of the Spanish.	
1680 Great Revolt against the Spanish. Pueblos continue.		
1825 First pioneers.		
1863		Gold discovered.
1865	Military presence.	
1875 Yavapai and Apache marched to reservation.		
1876 First settler in Oak Creek.		Mines in Black Hills.
1902 Sedona named. 20 Families.		Jerome mines thriving.
1950 Sedona Pop. 500.		Mines shut down.
1988 City Status, Pop. 12,500+		

after a series of explorations by an army officer of that name, it formed a major artery of communication for Europeans and Indians alike until the mid 19th century. Palatkwapi in the Hopi tongue means "The Place of the Red Rocks," and carries the story that it was once a dwelling place for several of the Hopi clans before their arrival on the Mesas. These migrating people, including the Bear, Parrot and Coyote clans, built a great cultural and religious center beside a river. However, life became too easy and the people became lazy and forgot their spirit nature. Eventually they were driven out by floods and in resuming their migrations, returned to their true selves.

Oswald "White Bear" Fredericks believes Palatkwapi was Palenque in Chiapas, Mexico; others say it was Casas Grandes in Chihuahua. But the name and the fact that at least some of the people dwelling in the Sedona area migrated north along the ancient trail to Hopi lands makes it possible that Palatkwapi was the Red Rock Country.

Jesse Walter Fewkes believed the close resemblance of the Verde Valley ruins to those of the Hopi and the similarity of the symbolism in pottery decoration supported the Hopi claim that some of their ancestors came from this region. The abandonment of many of the pueblos between 1300 and 1400 coincides with a period of major settlement on the Hopi Mesas. Whatever the case and wherever these people may have gone, after a period of intensive settlement by the Sinagua people, the Sedona area appears to have lain comparatively empty. Only occasionally was it used by the nomadic Yavapai and possibly the Apache.

The Yavapai

The story of the relationship between the indigenous Yavapai and the white people is not one that gives much credit to the latter. Once the Yavapai roamed over an area of 20,000 square miles in central and western Arizona. This territory ran approximately from the Salt and Gila rivers to the south, the Colorado river to the west, the Mogollon Rim to the east, and, the informants of E.W. Gifford who conducted the most detailed study of the people in the 1930's, stated that the country north of the Verde River to the San Francisco Mountains belonged to the Yavapai but none lived there. This included the Red Rock Country.

Today, the Yavapai are conspicuous by their absence and by the names of places that commemorate their demise: Skull Valley, Bloody Basin and the infamous Skeleton Cave. All were places where massacres by the army occurred. At Skeleton Cave on December 28th, 1872 many Yavapai families were killed by ricocheting bullets. To justify these murders the military described this as a splendid "battle" against "bloodthirsty Apache."

Army records from 1865 to 1875 reveal the killing of 700 Yavapai. This out of a total population estimated to be just over 2,000. The attitudes of miners and trappers to the native people were probably more brutal but the figures of deaths here are, of course, unrecorded.

In 1873 the remaining Yavapai were settled on the Camp Verde Reservation. They were very successful at digging irrigation ditches and cultivating the land. As a result of this and because of fear that the Yavapai might establish water rights, the white settlers sent delegates to Washington saying the Yavapai were Apache and should therefore be sent to the San Carlos Apache Reservation.

In the winter of 1875, General Crook acting under orders from Washington, marched 1400 Yavapai to San Carlos. This was the "March of Tears." No wagons were provided nor rest stops allowed. Many Yavapai were drowned in the crossing of rivers swollen by runoff from the melting of the

ANASAZI

NAVAJO

HOPI

PALATKWAPI-CHAVEZ TRAIL

COLORADO RIVER
HAVASUPAI
LITTLE
COLORADO
RIVER

WALAPAI

SAN FRANCISCO PEAKS
FLAGSTAFF ● ○ WALNUT CANYON
2 ○○ ● SEDONA
○3
1○
SINAGUA ○○6
MOHAVE ○○5
○7
PRESCOTT TONTO APACHE
MOGOLLON RIM
YAVAPAI VERDE

MOGOLLON

RIVER
Ft. McDowell
PHOENIX
SALT RIVER APACHE
MARICOPA
HOHOKAM
GILA RIVER
YUMA
PIMA

N

TUCSON ●

ARIZONA

50 MILES

1. TUZIGOOT
2. HONANKI
3. PALATKI
4. MONTEZUMA CASTLE
5. MONTEZUMA WELL
6. SACRED MT.
7. CLEAR CREEK

Map of the State of Arizona with inset square showing the location of the area covered by the maps in this book. The small circles mark the main centers - pueblos - of the Sinagua (Hakataya) in the Verde Valley. These centers as well as those of the surrounding Anasazi, Hohokam and Mogollon cultures declined and were abandoned by 1400. Within a few hundred years the subsequent native peoples: Yavapai, Apache, Pima, Hopi, Navajo, Mohave, etc. had established themselves in the general locations indicated on the map.

As a means of locating Sedona in a global context, a useful exercise may be to visualize it as being on a great circle, which, at a bearing of 37°45′ north of west, passes through Mount Shasta in northern California, Mount Fuji in Japan and Palenque in Mexico, on its way around the earth. This great circle is very close to 90° from the one going to Glastonbury mentioned on p. 32. It can best be appreciated in Sedona by observing Chimney Rock from the hills of the Airport Mesa or Bell Rock from Cathedral Rock. A bearing of 8°4′ to Mount Haleakala in Hawaii also passes through Ayers Rock (Uluru) in Australia and the Serpent Mound in Ohio before returning to Sedona. The great circle bearings given here and on p. 32 come from the exacting computer research of Terence R. Walsh.

mountain snow. Those unable to keep up were left behind or shot and left unburied.

Faced by the fact that the Yavapai were not Apache, Washington allowed many Yavapai to settle on the Fort McDowell Reservation in 1903. There they successfully resisted many attempts to remove them, including proposals in the late 1970's to flood the land with a dam. Two other small reservations were given, one in Prescott and one in Camp Verde.

The word "Yavapai" is thought by most authorities to translate as "the people of the Sun" - Enyaeva, "sun"; Pai, "people." As a nation, the Yavapai had occupied central and western Arizona from at least the 16th century. And, although their predecessors may have been the Sinagua, few traits appeared to have been carried over from them. There is no continuation of pueblo-type dwellings, for example. Yet a material discontinuity of this kind does not mean spiritual traditions are not carried over. It has been said that the "gods of one age become demons of the next." The point being that information, however transformed, is carried over and the Yavapai legends and traditions will carry remnants of the Sinaguan.

The Spanish expeditions of 1583 by Espejo and Luxan and that of 1604 by Onate tell of Indians they called "Cruzados" from crosses worn on the forehead. These were undoubtedly Yavapai (note the significance of the cross in the legends). But it is not until the 1800's that reliable information once again becomes available.

The Yavapai are classed as Yumans, sharing linguistic and cultural stock with the Walapai and the Havasupai. Yet these were their enemies. The Apache entered the region from the west sometime in the 18th century. Relations with the Yavapai were friendly. It was as a result of army pres-

sure in the 1860's that the Tonto Apache were forced into the Verde River region. From then on arose the confusion between the two groups.

The true Yavapai, as documented by E.W. Gifford, emerge as loosely affiliated bands of gatherer-hunters utilizing a wide resource area. Their traits include matrilineal descent, no civil chiefs (only leaders in times of war), buckskin clothing, cremation of the dead in their dwelling place, shamanistic and masked religious ceremony, sweat lodges and a goddess and her grandson as main tutelary and founding deities.

Caves were used for habitation in the winter months and thatched huts for traveling in summer. The main foods were mescal (agave), acorn, pinyon, walnuts, mesquite (one of the main sources being the Verde Valley), juniper berries, sunflower seeds, saguaro fruit, berries, deer and rabbits. Very little cultivation was done. The main tools were fashioned from bone, antler and flint. Arrows were used for hunting and clubs for war.

A subgroup of the northeastern Yavapai were known as the Wipukyipai or Wipukpa, meaning "those who dwell at the foot of the rocks or mountains." The mountains were the San Francisco Peaks. It is these people who were said by Jim Stacey, Gifford's main informant for the northeastern area, to have occupied an area that included the Red Rock Country and to have "descended Oak Creek to plant maize in moist land there."

Yavapai Legends

From the legends it is clear the Yavapai held the Red Rock Country in special regard. And probably, until under duress from the military, did not enter the canyons unless for a special and ceremonial purpose.

9

It was the emergence place of the goddess, Komwida-pokuwia or Kamalapukwia, whose name means "first person with medicine" or "old lady rock" - Komwida, "old woman"; Pokuwia, "black(?) stone medicine power." It was also the place of her grandson, Skatakaamcha or Sakarakaamche or Matinyaupakaamche, "light of day person on earth walking around," from whom much medicine power was derived.

For the following version of the creation legend we are indebted to *The Yavapai of Fort McDowell* edited by Sigrid Khera. It is told by Mike Harrison, born in 1886, and John Williams, born in 1904. It is entitled *How Everything Began and How We Learned to Live Right*.

The Coming to Sedona

We come out at Sedona, the middle of the world. This is our home. We call Sedona Wipuk. We call it after the rocks and the mountains there. All Yavapai come from Sedona. But in time they spread out.

North of Camp Verde there is Montezuma Well. This lake has no bottom and underneath the water spreads out wide. That's where the people come out first. Long time ago there was no water in that lake. And people were living down there... And there is one man, a little hummingbird, we call it "minamina" and it goes up... and it sees there is a good world up there.

So all the people they go up on a corn. They go around, go around, and where the ears of the corn come out between there they sleep. The turtle, he almost got caught up in there. He can't go fast. But he made it up. Lots of people come up from there, deer, quail, rabbits, jackrabbits... and when they look back the water is coming. The flood is in the well. But the water doesn't come out. He just stays level in there.

The corn that came out from Montezuma Well, we get the seeds from there first. Blue and white and red and black. After some time there comes another flood. The people put a girl in a hollow log. Put food in that log for her. Then they tell her, "The flood will raise you. You will hit the sky. But just lay still. If you lay still you will get out in the end." Then the people glued the log together with pitch.

The girl lay still in there all the time. After some time the water went down. The girl had a dove with her and she sent that dove out. The dove come back with a little weed. So the water has gone. There at Sedona is a high place. It is the highest place all around. And when the water went down, the log hit that high place. It stopped right there. And the girl came out from the log. That girl called Kamala-pukwia. Means "Old Lady White Stone." She is first woman and we come from her. She came out at Sedona and that's where all Indians come from.

The Birth of Sakarakaamche

Kamalapukwia lived in a cave in Sedona. She was all alone. One morning she ran over to Mingus Mountain. Lay down there before the sun came up. The sun comes up and hits her inside. After that she went to that cave where water drips down all the time. She lay down and the water came down and hit her. Made her a baby. A little girl.

When that girl came to age, Kamalapukwia said to her, "Daughter, they did that and you come up. You go over there and do like I did." The girl said, "All right." She went up to Mingus Mountain and lay down there. That's the highest mountain around there and that's where the sun comes first in the morning. But the sun did not hit her. Then her mother said, "Run down over there where the water drips, at the cave in Sedona. Lay under there, same way you did up on the mountain." So the girl did. She went to the cave where

the water drips down and lay under. The water came, but he saw it is his daughter. So he stopped the water halfways.

The girl told that to her mother. The old lady said, "We'll fix it. Next morning you go up on mountain again and I help you." Before sun comes up the girl lay there and old woman on top of her. When sun comes out, the old woman quickly moved aside and he hits the girl. Then they go over where the water drips down in cave. Old woman made the girl lay down and she was laying on top. When the water came down, she pulled over and it went into girl. She got pregnant and got the little baby, it was a boy: Sakarakaamche.

The Giving of Medicine

When that boy was still a baby, a bad eagle killed his mother. The eagle saw the lady down there, came down and got her. Now there were only two people; the old lady Kamalapukwia and the little boy Sakarakaamche. The old lady raised the little boy.

The old lady, she told Sakarakaamche everything. Teach him everything. And he learned from his father, the Cloud. He knew everything about all the weeds which cure all the sicknesses. He learned about the weeds from the old lady, his grandmother. We don't know where she learned it, but Sakarakaamche learned it from her. And he is the one who is teaching the humans who come up.

There is a cave in Sedona with lots of marks on the wall. Sakarakaamche made those marks. He took the people in there and gave them the right songs. Teach them dances. Some people listened well to what Sakarakaamche said... and some didn't. He tried to teach the Yavapai something, but we didn't listen well. We didn't get much. One thing he gave us, a stick with a string on it. That's the bow and arrow. And he gave us two little sticks like pliers to pick the cactus fruit. But

he gave us four sacred things. He gave us the black root, we call it isamaganyach, the yellow powder, we call it atchitawsa, the blue stone and the white stone.

Black root is a very great medicine. It helps against pains and sores. It makes you feel good again. The yellow powder is the pollen from the cattail. The medicine man, when he heals somebody, he puts yellow powder on him. Yellow powder stands for the light. It helps you think and talk right. The blue stone and the white stone, that's what protects us from bad things. The blue stone for men, the white stone for the women. When you have these stones and think well, bad things can't hit you.

Sakarakaamche teach us everything. He teach us how to pray, how to sing right, how to dance. My people used to sing every morning. Before they do anything, they sing. When they sing, they pray and things come out right. My people don't read or write. They have no song book. But they know how to sing. They have it in their heart. They get it from Sakarakaamche.

The blue stone is turquoise, the white stone is quartz. The next account of the creation legend comes from Violla Jimulla whose parents made the March of Tears in 1875. Her life story was told by Franklin Barnett in *Violla Jimulla: The Indian Chieftess.*

The Four Worlds

The legend about the creation of the Yavapai Indians is based upon four different cycles or worlds. The first people emerged from underground and were removed from the earth by a flood. The second world was the time of the Goddess Komwida Pokwee (Old Woman Rock) and her grandson Skatakaamcha. The third ended by world fire and we live in the fourth today.

Komwida Pokwee, as a girl, came from the flood and settled in the Red Rock Country near what is now Sedona. She is the Goddess of the supernatural and medicine powers, and is beautiful and as pure as a downy white feather. Skatakaamcha is her grandson, and all of the songs, supernatural powers, and medicine power and knowledge were given to him by his grandmother, and were passed on to the Yavapai medicine men and their people. The medicine men, or anyone believing in the religion, may see her yet in a vision or dream and receive instructions, comfort and encouragement. These two, together, always set a good example for our Yavapai people to follow.

This last account of the origin tale is related by E.W. Gifford in his work on the Southeastern Yavapai (1932). His source was Mike Burns, born around 1860.

The People of the Sun

In the beginning people lived in the Underworld. A great tree grew there which pierced the sky of the Underworld. Up this people climbed into this world, but failed to close the hole. Water gushed up through the hole, flooding this world and drowning the people.

Someone had hollowed out a great pine tree, into which a woman named Komwidapokuwia entered and was sealed in with pitch. She took with her food enough for a number of years, also some birds. She was instructed not to look out until the log lay perfectly still.

After a long time Komwidapokuwia sent out a dove through a small opening. After two days it returned with a dry bit of plant in its beak. Then she knew the flood was over. She emerged from her log which had stranded on San Francisco Mountain. She then went south to the Red Rock country on the east side of the Verde River.

There she bore a daughter, begotten by the sun, who had fertilized her in the following way. There was a dripping spring, where she lay in the early morning. Just at sunrise water dripped into her at the same instant as the sun's rays touched it. She bore a daughter, who is the firstborn child in this world. Eventually the girl became pregnant and bore a son who was named Amchitapuka, "first man on earth."

Two days after the birth Komwidapokuwia instructed her daughter to collect wood. While she was out a great eagle swooped upon her and carried her to his rocky aerie, where she was devoured by the eaglets. Komwidapokuwia then had to care for her grandson, who grew to be a young man. He became a great man. Some say he became a rock in the Red Rock Country. His footprints, made in soft mud, turned to rock and are now to be seen.

Another version includes seeds in the hollow log, and stories of how Komwidapokuwia made the trees, animals and people to repopulate the world. These people were identified as the pueblo builders. The footprints of Amchitapuka or Skatakaamcha are said to be in the rocks around the source of Oak Creek. Some say - not Yavapai - that it is he and his grandmother who stand back to back in Cathedral Rock. Other sources say that an old woman presence now abides in the Boynton Canyon area.

The following legends of Komwidapokuwia and her grandson come from Gifford's later and more complete work (1936). His principle source was Jim Stacey who was described as aged (he died in 1933) and who still dwelt in caves in the traditional way. The text refers to a blind shaman, the Muukyat, otherwise called Jim. Muukyat recorded many shaman's songs in 1932, the references for which appear in the bibliography. The translations are by Johnson Stacey, son of Jim Stacey, but they had been edited by Gifford into a very prosaic form. I have therefore taken the liberty to present them in a more poetic way, while, I hope, resurrecting a little more of the original spirit with which they were told. Great thanks must go to E.W. Gifford for the use of his material. It was stated several times by the medicine men that just telling these stories would bring rain.

The Giving of the Songs

Komwidapokuwia and Skatakaamcha were semacha. They established many features of Yavapai culture and were patron deities of shamans. Red Rock Country was once their home. Later, goddess went to dwell in northern sky and Skatakaamcha in southern. No one sees them on earth now except shamans.

A curing shaman was called basemacha: ba, person; semacha, deities. Power to cure got from goddess and especially from her grandson, who bestowed gourd rattle for curing. His singing cured people all over the world.

Komwidapokuwia's hair hung to her knees, and shone like stars. She gave Muukyat the song that he sang next. It was for curing all kinds of illness. This is a way of singing, like this...

The Songs of Komwidapokuwia

Pukmukwana, black stone powder grinding around,
Wove and talked into existence the girl
                        Komwidapokuwia.
She came into existence and sang like this:

In the white morning
In the white morning
The small star in heaven wove.
In the morning, the small morning
It wove and made heaven.

After she had sung a little while, it became
White all over the world.
The girl came forth and stood and sang.
Heaven was used for her body.
She shook her rattle
And from its power it became white
All over the world.
That was White Morning Road.
Pukmukwana had woven and talked
Into existence the girl Komwidapokuwia.

Star powder heaven was used for her body
She came forth and stood and sang:

My talking and singing are life.
I speak for spiritual life
All over the world.
I speak and all the world
Lightens up to heaven.
This is the way I sing
When I listen to the songs of heaven.

Small heaven with white circles her chest was woven of,
She sang to make different all the world.
This she sang for the sake of the shamans.
She sang and flowers bloomed in the sky.
This is her way of singing:

My songs were made for the beautiful sky.
My word went out into the sky.
The world stood still.
A rainbow from heaven reached to this world.
Everything was still.
My song changed everything.

This is the way I sang when I was in the world
Going around in the Red Rock Country.

As he sang Muukyat raised his hand as did Komwida-pokuwia, from whose four fingers light ascended to heaven. He shook the gourd rattle with his right hand.

> The light from my fingers
> Strikes the heavens like thunder
> And it rains.

There now follows the song of Skatakaamcha and with it the story of how he wished to visit his fathers. Even though Komwidapokuwia told him this was a very hard thing to do he wanted to do it anyway. He went over the ocean to visit Sun and Cloud by walking on Spider's Web. Sun put medicine in the right side of his body and then Cloud put medicine in the left side. "Sun and Cloud were my fathers, because of the fertilizing waters and sunbeam that had entered my mother."

The Songs of Skatakaamcha

Skatakaamcha sang:

> They gave me four lines of lightning
> To descend to earth.
> Two on the left belonged to Cloud
> Two on the right belonged to Sun.
> I descended on the lightning flashes.
> I arrived at Komwidapokuwia's place.
> I knelt on the ground, and pressed.
> With my hands and my knees I pressed
> On the ground and sang.
> When I lifted my hands
> Medicine plants sprouted out of the earth.

Muukyat sang the song he heard Skatakaamcha sing. Pressing on the ground he could not use his rattle. Then, coming through the air, Skatakaamcha sang:

> I have made good things in this world.
> Now I am going to cross over the river.
> I'll be singing as I go under the heavens.
> The thunder will sound
> The lightning will split my body
> And four parts will go in each direction.
> Somewhere in heaven is another people
> For me to teach.
> I will make new shamans.
> There are only new shamans now.
> They will cure all disease by singing.

This is the way Skatakaamcha sings when he walks: he picks up the white dawn powder and makes a cross on his chest and speaks of it. He calls it the Morning Cross. He does this as he walks. He turns back and comes out of heaven and speaks to the world and heaven. Heaven and earth are lost in a hard rainstorm. The earth has dew on it. All over the world people feel happy.

He stood on the dawn as he spoke and sang:

> Dark Medicine Boy and I sang
> As we climbed to heaven.
> We sang like this together as we went.
> On my right side Sun made Dark Medicine Signs.
> We sang like this as the spots were made.
> And half my body was the Sun.
> On my left side Cloud made Lightning Signs.
> We sang like this as the lines were made.
> From heaven to earth went the four lines.
> Two lines of Dark Medicine Lightning from Sun.
> Two lines of Thunder Lightning from Cloud.
> I traveled down the lines of lightning to the earth.
> I sang this song as I knelt and pressed
> My hands into the earth.
> Dark Medicine plant grew up out of the ground.

When he knelt and pressed on the ground he sang as I am singing now. As he sank into the ground Dark Medicine grew up. It grew up with beautiful flowers upon it. All the people over here were saying what good medicine it was.

Skatakaamcha said:

> It is my heart
> My heart and spirit together.
> Together, I plant it out under
>   the heavens
> For you people.
> If you sing like this you will
>   keep alive.

Skatakaamcha said to the people in the Red Rock Country:

> You open me down the middle
> From my head to my crotch,
> And turn me belly down upon
>   the ground
> Then sing around my body
> And you will get my songs.
> If you sing my songs you will
>   keep alive.

Through remembering the ancient legends we bring the world to life. If the songs are not sung and the myths are not told, then the land will die.

The Twin Buttes.

Chapter 2

GEOMANCY

There seem to be certain favored places on the earth where its magnetic and even more subtle forces are most powerful and most easily felt by persons susceptible to such things.

J.D. Evans Wentz. 1911.

Geomythics

Geomancy is the divination of the spirit of the place - the "Earth Spirit." Geomantic knowledge embraces the geography, the natural and the human history and the geometric and spiritual dimensions of a particular place or an area of the earth. It includes study of the flora and fauna, the climate and the local magnetic and electrical fields. It attempts to explain their relationship to adjacent natural features, to heavenly bodies, to underground currents and to the nature invested in the place by human activities.

This latter is especially important, for what humans do to or think about a place affects its properties. Has the primordial landscape remained unaffected, or has it been altered by successive waves of settlers moving through it, each bringing their agriculture, their technologies, their dwellings, their notions of the sacred, their passions and their wars? Burial grounds, walls and hedges, temples, sites of battles and roads are a few examples of the way the geomantic properties of humanly inhabited landscapes evolve. It is extraordinary how the basic elemental signature of a place can be altered by generations of human habitation. Rivers can be diverted, hills leveled, forests cleared and even climates changed.

A branch of geomancy known as geomythics focuses on the ideas, the myths or the stories held about a place and illustrates how human thinking can determine its character. Mount Ararat in eastern Turkey for example, is held in human minds as the place of the landing of The Ark after the world flood. The stories of the world-creating acts of the Australian dreamtime ancestors, or of the heroes of the ancient Celtic world, determine how a place is named and how it will be perceived in the minds of future generations. This is geomythics. The interaction of the nature of the place with the properties of the cognitive faculties of the mind generates a spirit presence which may then be seen to exist in a realm independent of both.

Forests, canyons or caves may be invested with elemental or divine inhabitants whose presence may become more powerful by successive tellings of their myth or by the building of shrines or other structures dedicated to them. In this way spirit presence can assume an existence independent of its geomantic location and can achieve archetypal significance in a universal mind. Yahweh, for example, began life as a thunder god of a mountain. Athena, as an owl spirit living in rock crevices in a region of Anatolia.

The question to be asked about the Red Rock Country is this: who invested what myths in which places when?

Names are an excellent way to begin the understanding of a location's geomantic powers. Wherever the Indian names and legends can be discovered in the Sedona area entranceways to the geomythical realm can be found. Many of the present day names are too mundane to interact

Courthouse Rock from the northwest.

creatively with the elemental properties of the landscape and the deeper cognitive faculties of the mind. Coffee Pot Rock, for example, or Steamboat Rock for all their homeliness, pale before the geomythic potentials of "Horus Rock" or "Thunderbird Rock." And the naming of Soldier Pass after a trooper who was buried there is probably at odds with the nature of the valley and will fail to bring out its full geomantic potential.

Names like Devil's Bridge, Devil's Kitchen and Devil's Dining Room are clues to a deeper, underlying geomantic power. Often an overlying and, in this case, Christian culture attributes what it fears most to a place it senses carries power through from an earlier time. Sometimes it is with cause - the sinkholes are dangerous places. Sometimes it

is without a cause other than the wish to suppress the mystery of the unknown.

The name of Courthouse Rock expresses a specific idea which may have its origin in a deeper past. It is said, although this may be apocryphal, that the Indians went there to settle disputes. Whether this is true or not does not really matter. An idea or a place does not have to have an antique origin to authenticate it. The name, Courthouse Rock, aptly embodies the spirit of the place, that of the law, and this will deepen and continue to grow as more actions and thoughts resonating with this spirit are invested within it.

Capitol Butte is an example of a place struggling to find a name which expresses its spirit. To some people it is "Gray Mountain" or "Old Grayback" with a definite feminine association. It is said that the Indians called it and the peaks around it "Thunder Mountain," perhaps because it attracted many lightning strikes being at the center of a wide area. On the summit of the ridge running west from Old Grayback is a rock known as Lizard Head, the head of a lizard being clearly visible. It was pointed out to me by a guide, Rahelio, that this rock undergoes a metamorphosis when seen from the north. It then takes on the outline of the head of a bald eagle. Such figures have ancestral legends attached to them among native peoples.

Much confusion arises in Sedona through either the transference of place names or the lack of names altogether. Sedona is a new landscape for the people still finding their home within it. This is unlike the situation in Europe where every feature has a name and very likely a story steeped within the past. Though perhaps it does not matter if places in Sedona remain unnamed, it is hoped that names, when they are found, will resonate with the intrinsic sacred properties that are felt by many to be present in this place of the red earth.

The Yavapai Names

If the name of a place can reveal so much, is there any significance in the name of Sedona itself? We know the Yavapai called the area Wipuk, "at the foot of the rocks and mountains," and that Pukwia means "medicine stone," so it seems likely that it was considered to be a place of medicine power, but what does the apparently arbitrary naming of Sedona signify?

The name Sedona arose in 1902 after T.C. Schnebly, one of the first settlers, had Oak Creek Station rejected as the name for a post office permit. It was too long. It is said that in a moment of inspiration he named the station after his wife Sedona.

There has already been some speculation on this unusual name. It has been pointed out that written backwards Sedona spells anodes, the positive pole of an electrical source such as a battery. I, personally, prefer a meaning based upon a Spanish translation. Dona is a term of respect employed before the Christian name of a woman, for example, Dona Christina. The equivalent for a man would be Don. Se is a pronoun used before her, him, you or them, meaning to her, to him, etc. It also means himself, herself or even each other. However, its most common meaning is simply "to know." Sedona, therefore, could mean to know the respected woman or to know and respect the place of the woman.

On this subject, the 19th century traveler, Hiram Hodge, gives the following story which he says came from "old Aztec traditions."

The earth is the offspring of the sky. Long prior to the present race of men, the earth was peopled by a race of giants who in time died off, leaving the earth uninhabited. After a long time, a celestial virgin, a child of one of the 13 great deities who rule all things, came down to earth, and being well-pleased, remained. Once, when in a deep sleep, a drop of dew fell on her and she conceived and bore two children, a son and a daughter, from whom have sprung all the people of the earth. The name of this celestial virgin was Arizunna, the beautiful, or sun-beloved maiden.

Hodge wrote that in the language of the Mohave, "Ari" meant sun as well as holy, good and beautiful, and "Urnia" meant maiden. Thus, the possible translation of Arizona in the Mohave tongue would be "the good and beautiful sun maiden." He preferred this to the "Arid Zone" from the Spanish, but accepted that either was possible.

If the two words, Sedona and Arizona were put together and considerable liberty taken in the translation, we could then arrive at a meaning which approximates: "to know the sacred and beautiful place of the sun-beloved maiden." This ties in very well with the Yavapai legend of Komwida-pokuwia who was impregnated by the sun after her arrival in the area now known as Sedona.

19

To return at this point to the Yavapai legends, it is said that the presence of a deity is to be found in the form of a rock or in footprints in the rock. The name Komwidapokuwia itself means "old woman rock." An essential part of the legend of Skatakaamcha is how he impressed himself upon the rocks and can be found by singing his songs.

Of particular concern in the legends is the imagery

Cathedral Rock and Oak Creek.

of sky and earth and the connecting of the two, especially by means of a lightning flash. This provides the pathway for deities or their powers to travel on in southwestern traditions. We could therefore expect the Yavapai names of the prominent features of the Red Rock Country to bear reference to the acts of Komwidapokuwia and Skatakaamcha, especially where they formed the bridge between the worlds.

Underground Water

The art of geomancy grew into a highly refined state in China where it was known as Feng-Shui or "Wind-Water." It taught that for the essential life force or Ch'i to flow harmoniously there had to be a balance of the elements and of Yin and Yang, the two cosmic forces of the White Tiger and the Blue Dragon. Places that were excessively Yang or excessively Yin were seen as not particularly suitable for habitation but they could be brought into balance by application of standard geomantic practices.

Cathedral Rock is an example of a place where Yin and Yang forces have been brought into balance through the action of the elements. The spires and domes of this beautiful formation evoke the qualities of a cathedral and it is well worth the scramble to climb up to them. At first glance the towering rocks appear to be Yang in their quality, but as one ascends, the actions of water become particularly noticeable. The round, smooth, red Supai bedrock has been sculpted into massive piers at the summit. For millions of years Oak Creek has made its way down from the springs of the Mogollon Rim, carving the deep, lush canyon that bears its name. Flowing through many different courses it eroded away the layers of stone before finding its present course. The western flanks of Cathedral Rock reveal several different levels at which the river once flowed. Because of the continued presence of Oak Creek at its foot, Cathedral Rock in terms of Feng-Shui, is a place where the Yin and Yang forces meet in balance and establish terrestrial harmony.

One important aspect of geomancy is the presence of flowing underground water. This can give rise to spectacular formations such as caverns and sinkholes, and to the otherwise invisible presence of strong Yin energies on the surface above. Classic evidence for the presence of underground flowing water - not simply water sitting in the water table - is provided by several features in the area.

First, variation of land elevation is provided by the Colorado Plateau lying to the north of the Sedona area. Sedona sits below the edge of a vast rainwater collector.

Second, suitable conditions for the creation of aquifers - underground water channels of any size - in the bedrock is provided by the underlying layers of limestone and sandstone. Limestone is permeable and easily cut by water. The Redwall Limestone on which the Red Rock Country sits is fragmented by faults through which the water is drawn. A good example of a fault is provided by Oak Creek Canyon. An indication of fissures in the bedrock is the large number of faults filled by volcanic lava. In places the basaltic volcanic material has filled overground stream channels and is certain to have filled ones underground. Some fissures which remain open are said to be breathing holes for the San Francisco Peaks, and the volume of air expelled and drawn in at regular periods suggests a vast subterranean system of tunnels and caverns. It is probable there are three main levels of water concentration below Sedona corresponding to porous geological strata.

Finally, evidence of large aquifers is demonstrated by the existence of visible caverns, powerful springs and sinkholes. The springs which give rise to Oak Creek emerge from fault fractures in the cliff walls with great strength, indicating many miles of subterranean activity. Granddad's or Grandma's Cave lies above Harding Spring in Oak Creek Canyon and is probably a former underground water channel. There are two sinkholes, or cenotes, close to Sedona and one a few miles to the west.

A sinkhole is formed by the movement of underground water eroding soft rock in such a way that a circular cavern is formed. This is through the dissolving of particles of soft rock until the weight of rock above cannot be supported and collapses. The Devil's Kitchen is a sinkhole some 60 feet deep and over 100 feet across. The roof fell in sometime in the 1880's. The Devil's Dining Room is some 75 feet deep and 25 feet across, and the third sinkhole south of Boynton Pass on Jackass Flats is approaching 100 feet in depth. That these sinkholes no longer contain water, unlike Montezuma Well, a sinkhole to the southeast, indicates that the underground streams have dropped to a deeper level. It is possible that these streams emerge at Page Springs to the south. Further evidence for underground streams would be provided by either objective hydrological research or by subjective divining work on the ground or from maps.

Turning to the second method, water diviners report that a specific charge, negative in polarity, is associated with the presence of underground water. This would appear to correspond to the qualities of Ch'i characterized as Yin in Feng-Shui. Once attuned to, this energy can be followed by the diviner, even though the stream may be thousands of feet below the surface. At this depth the water is likely to be what is known as the earth's "primary water" as opposed to "secondary water" which is the water recycled in the oceans, rivers and rain.

Primary water is that solution which, present in the elemental soup that forms the magma and the earth's core, is forced up by super-temperatures and pressures, until, after deposition and crystallization of its mineral substances, it emerges as water on the earth's surface. It generally has a high mineral content, is often hot and has a constant rate and quantity of flow. An example of this is Montezuma Well where the 76 degree water carries a high percentage of dissolved limestone. The intuitive understanding of Montezuma Well possessing an extremely deep source is expressed in local legends of swimmers being drowned and their bodies never recovered.

Water diviners report that primary water is driven upwards until it reaches an impermeable layer of stone where it branches out laterally in several veins. The point on the surface of the earth above the point where the water meets the impermeable layer is known as a "blind spring" and the point below is known as a "dome."

Blind springs do not have to be formed solely by primary water. If conditions are right secondary water can pass deeply enough into the earth to be driven out from a great depth elsewhere. The geological layers of the Colorado Plateau produce circumstances ideal for the creation of blind springs. If the theory of vast caverns filled with water in the center of the plateau is correct then this has the potential to create a place of negative polarity or Yin energy on an almost unimaginable scale.

A blind spring is an extremely powerful confluence of Yin energy that can be depicted on the earth's surface in the two-dimensional form of a spiral, in the three-dimensional form of a cone and in the four-dimensional form as a complex set of interpenetrating auric sheaves. These may be said to be power centers, places where Yang energy - especially lightning - converges; and where among people sensitive to these energies, ceremonies were performed and temples such as stone circles or pyramids constructed.

Because currents of Yin energy on the surface generated by water flowing underground carry a negative polarity in relation to the energies of the human body, they are often popularly known as "black streams." This is quite misleading. Although it is not advisable to site a house or to sleep over an underground stream as energy is being earthed and carried away, this situation in itself is not harmful and can be prevented by simple techniques that the diviner who found the stream would be familiar with. A black stream, (in terms of Feng-Shui a place where Ch'i has been converted to Sha - noxious vapors) is where the energy does not move at all and remains stagnant. There are not many places of Sha in such a dynamic landscape as the Red Rock Country.

Just a word on Yang energies (which will be dealt with again in the chapter on Ley Lines), or positively charged energy. The sharp mountainous landscape of Sedona, the towering red buttes, the extremely high incidence of lightning strikes in the summer, the number of geomagnetic anomalies and the powerful sun all indicate the sort of electrical activity characterized by the Blue Dragon energies of Feng-Shui.

Yang energies are inseparable from Yin energies. Together with the five elements they form the breath of Ch'i, the one-life energy in all its multitudinous aspects. It would be truer to say "there is more Yin in this place" than "this place is Yin." In the same way as wind does not "blow" but rather rushes from one place to another seeking to balance areas of different pressure, a better image of Ch'i would be one where the energies are seen to ebb and flow and even exchange polarities, or at least be seen as dynamic movement instead of fixity.

The underground water energies, according to geomantic principles, are essential for the proper balancing of energies upon the surface. Places where the White Tiger is strong brings the Blue Dragon down to earth and assures harmony and well-being. The presence of huge lakes in subterranean chambers would create a polarity which skilled geomancers could work with to bring this fusion about. In a landscape like Sedona the atmospheric Blue Dragon energy is extremely volatile. If there were to be a period of drought the absence of Yin energy would mean that the violent electrical storms of summer would scorch the earth and create disharmony.

Some archaeologists think this situation occurred in the late 13th century when the Southwest experienced a prolonged period of drought. Rivers like Oak Creek and the Colorado are deceptive. The great canyons in which they lie make them appear to be powerful. However, the actual volume of water they carry is relatively small. These great canyons are a result of faulting and many millions of years of erosion and their rivers arise in the midst of desert lands of little rain.

For several decades beginning around the year 1275 the rain and snow did not come to the Colorado Plateau. It is thought that the aquifers and rivers slowly dwindled to a trickle and then ceased to flow. By 1350 the pueblos of the Sinagua were abandoned and the complex irrigation systems lay useless. There was always some water but the pueblo lifeway had become too successful. With villages of 40 rooms on an average of every two miles down Beaver Creek there was simply not enough water to go around when the creek dried up. The plant cover died back and the Yang energies raged overhead in summer with nothing to bring down the rain. The Sinagua fulfilled the name given to them and moved on.

Further south, in the Hohokam farming lands, the low level of the Salt and Gila rivers could not fill the many miles of irrigation canals and the overspecialized and canal dependent agricultural system collapsed. In the Pima language, Hohokam means "exhausted people," people exhausted by the struggle for declining sources of water.

On the other hand, although we know from tree-ring analysis that 1275 to 1350 were extremely dry years, it cannot be proven that drought was the sole reason for the "disappearance" of the Sinagua, the Hohokam and the Anasazi. If the Hopi legends of the migrations have historical accuracy then it could be that the ancestors of those peoples were responding to spiritual imperatives rather than purely material and climactic ones. Perhaps the Ch'i energy was not moving as it should and the lack of response to the rain ceremonies signified the need for migration rather than the need for migration arising because of the lack of rain.

Today in Arizona a similar picture prevails. The population has become very successful in establishing itself, in exploiting water resources, in living in a desert. So successful at harnessing the energy of the Colorado River in fact, that if the total net demands made upon it were realized simultaneously they would far exceed the volume of water. It has been many years since the waters of the river have regularly flowed into the sea.

In some parts of Arizona where the water table is extensive and uniform, for example around Black Mesa in Hopi-Navajo land, it has been calculated that 1000 years of rain are necessary to add two inches to the water table. Pumping from wells has reduced the water table by 20 inches in about as many years. It is true that runoff has been captured in many places and no longer erodes the soil but if there is no rain there will be nothing for irrigation. Also, the gains here are more than offset by the last 100 years of unlimited cattle grazing. The descriptions of the quality of original grassland in Arizona indicate that the fragile desert ecology has been drastically altered by cattle grazing. Many deep gullies have recently been made. Conditions have been prepared for disaster given a period of drought and tempestuous storms as is known to have happened at least once before.

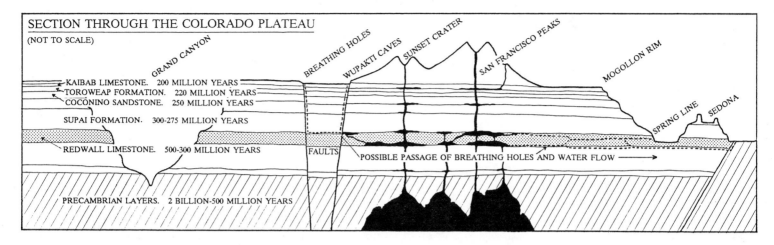

SECTION THROUGH THE COLORADO PLATEAU
(NOT TO SCALE)

GRAND CANYON — BREATHING HOLES — WUPAKTI CAVES — SUNSET CRATER — SAN FRANCISCO PEAKS — MOGOLLON RIM — SPRING LINE — SEDONA

KAIBAB LIMESTONE. 200 MILLION YEARS
TOROWEAP FORMATION. 220 MILLION YEARS
COCONINO SANDSTONE. 250 MILLION YEARS
SUPAI FORMATION. 300-275 MILLION YEARS
REDWALL LIMESTONE. 500-300 MILLION YEARS
FAULTS
POSSIBLE PASSAGE OF BREATHING HOLES AND WATER FLOW →
PRECAMBRIAN LAYERS. 2 BILLION-500 MILLION YEARS

The Breathing Holes

This simplified section through the Colorado Plateau demonstrates a possible model for the passage of underground water and for an unusual cavern system created by volcanic activity. This is suggested by the presence of "breathing holes" around the San Francisco Peaks. The holes ring the peaks with several at Wupatki and one, I have been told but have not seen, in the Sedona area. Analysis of air movement through the holes indicates huge subterranean caverns, so large that one explanation for the movement of air through them includes the pull of the moon on a body of underground water. The holes are said to inhale and exhale every six hours with the movement of the moon. Whatever the explanation, the holes help generate an unusual pattern of micro-climates in the area, knowledge of which may have been utilized by the Native Americans in ceremonial-technological, weather-changing activity.

It is also unusual that the water table under the Colorado Plateau lifts to a height out of proportion to the lifting of the land below the part of the Black Mesa where the main Hopi villages are located. There is no straightforward hydrological explanation for this rise in the level of the water table. It is as though the presence of the people on the Mesas has somehow drawn the water up.

In geomantic terms the combined elements of this system relate in a specialized dependency where alteration to any part could effect the movement of the Ch'i and imperil the fragile desert ecology. The strip mining of Black Mesa, for example, and the emptying of the aquifers there may upset the balance of the system. Springs could dry up. There is even a remote chance volcanic activity could resume or drought, deforestation and erosion take place. It is hard for us today with the split between our logical, scientific brains and our intuitive, spirit selves to comprehend the techniques employed by native peoples to work with the elemental powers. We would call those techniques "magic" and dismiss them. But if we do, we drive the magical component out of our own technology. It all depends on our approach. As the author of Needles of Stone, Tom Graves, loves to ask, "What is the difference between magical technology and technological magic?"

Chapter 3

GEOMANTIC HARMONIES AND LEY LINES

The roots of all living things are tied together.
When the... forest is destroyed... the world will end.
Chan K'in Viejo. Elder of the Lacandon Maya.

Feng-Shui and Sedona

Feng-Shui is the name of the Chinese system of geomancy. The word means "Wind-Water" which hints at the subtlety of its nature. It is hard to grasp and, like the breath, is always in a pattern of flow and movement.

Feng-Shui is concerned with energy or Ch'i, and with the balance among forces. The two primary forces are Yin and Yang, symbolized by the White Tiger and the Blue Dragon. These two forces flow in currents around the landscape, following courses known as lung mei or "dragon veins." Yang energy will arise in rough, mountainous terrain and often following a ridge - a dragon vein - will flow down and meet its inseparable counterpart, the Yin energy, in the surrounding plains and foothills. Where the two forces meet in a harmonious proportion will be a place conducive to health and good fortune.

Where the land is flat, all Yin, the Ch'i will have difficulty in achieving balance so pagodas might be built or trees planted to help the land breathe again. The inbreath and the outbreath of Yang and Yin seek balance, and in their movement give rise to other forms of Ch'i, the five elements: water, earth, metal, wood and fire. The subtle interplay of all these forces gives rise to the different types of landform which may be more or less beneficial to life.

A rounded peak corresponds to the element metal, to Venus and ideally lies in the west. A flattened peak corresponds to wood, to Jupiter and should lie to the east. A plateau corresponds to earth, to Saturn and should lie near the center of the area. A sharp peak corresponds to fire, to Mars and should lie to the south. A wavy ridge corresponds to water, to Mercury and ideally lies to the north.

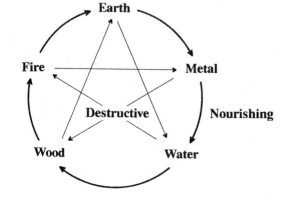

Figure 1.

25

The five elements relate to each other in a system of mutual nourishment or destruction as shown in Figure 1. The circle represents nourishing and the arrows represent destructive relationships. The perfectly balanced place where all influences combine for maximum benefit would be where the forms of the land approximate in direction and shape the pattern shown in Figure 2. It can be seen that the most volatile relationships of fire and water and metal and wood are kept distanced by the central plateau of earth.

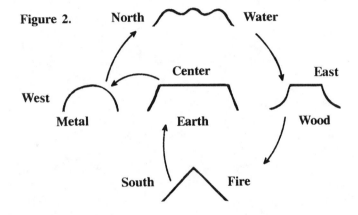

Figure 2.

Let's examine the relationships of Ch'i surrounding the most obvious example of a central plateau in the Sedona area, the Airport Mesa or Tabletop Mountain. (Please refer to Figure D on the main map of this chapter.) Here Old Grayback forms a rounded peak corresponding to metal or Venus. However, instead of being in its ideal place to the west, the peak lies to the north. The flat-topped peak adjacent to the Airport Mesa corresponds to the form of wood or Jupiter and falls in its ideal place to the east. Examples of sharp peaks are all around but not one stands out more clearly than does Bell Rock which thus corresponds to fire or Mars, and lies in its ideal place to the south. This leaves the wavy, undulating lines of the western landscape around Scheurman Mountain to correspond to

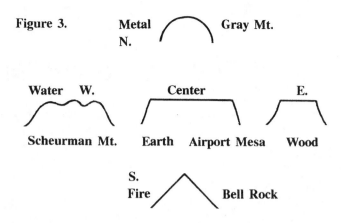

Figure 3.

the element of water or Mercury, which is out of its ideal place, the North.

The shape of the hills around the Airport Mesa appear to correspond well to the ideal with three of the five elements falling in their correct places. This would seem to be fairly beneficent. But because of the place of water being taken by metal and metal by water some disharmony arises. Water will have difficulty in nourishing wood as indicated by the curved arrows in Figure 4. And wood is threatened by its proximity to metal as indicated by the straight arrows.

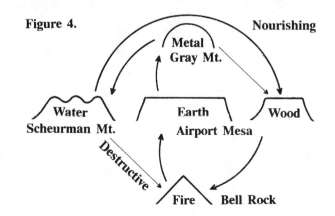

Figure 4.

The element corresponding to wood or Jupiter, is weakened by lack of nourishment from the element of water, which in turn is weakened by its proximity to fire - both features of a hot climate where none but semi-desert plants survive. Wood is also threatened by metal which signifies a general wasting away or a possible injury. This situation can be prevented through appropriate actions. It would not be appropriate for instance to build a pagoda on Scheurman Mountain or to undulate the peak of Old Grayback to induce them to reverse their correspondences. It would be appropriate to pay attention to the water table in the area and to watch the use of metal; for example, it would be beneficial to use wholly natural materials in building and to accommodate and nurture the existing trees. As the Hohokam and the Sinagua discovered at great cultural cost around 1300, all their technology and irrigation systems were useless in the desert land if the rain and snow did not fall. To be forewarned is to be forearmed.

The mei, the lines of Yin or Yang energy, often follow the contours in their movements around the land. At the points where they cross each other the Ch'i force then disperses or collects. A Yang hill in a Yin plain or a Yin plateau in rugged Yang terrain would be places where the Ch'i would gather. The White Tiger breathes most deeply where it is complemented by the Blue Dragon, and vice-versa. Where the energy cannot move at all it becomes Sha, literally "noxious exhalations," and is a source of ill-health and misfortune. Again, it can be remedied through obvious balancing practices which fall within the scope of those with aesthetic eyes or sound common sense. Don't build in a place where the sun cannot reach, the air cannot circulate and the water cannot drain away.

These are examples of the Chinese geomantic tradition of Feng-Shui which can now lead us to a further practice, not uncomplementary, drawn from European examples.

Ley Lines

There are two types of lines that can be described as leys. Both are alignments across the landscape but one carries a purpose whereas the other is merely a line. An example of the latter would be a highway that was aligned to a mountain peak before entering a city and terminating at a public monument. In the 18th century such alignments were all the rage in Europe. Tree-lined views would extend from the grand houses of the aristocracy to a folly or a natural feature on a distant hill. Such leys quickly disappear as their features erode. The other kind of alignment is similarly a product of intention but also has an elemental basis. It can be found to carry a charge of energy independent of the human features used to mark its path. This would correspond to the lung mei of Feng-Shui and to the megalithic alignments of Europe.

Some have described these lines as the etheric network of the earth or the planetary grid. It is the subtle energy of these lines, detectable by divining techniques, that has so fascinated geomancers and inspired the placing of markers at key points in the system. It has further inspired the creation of microcosmic representations of these patterns in temples, stone circles and holy cities.

Through the principles of sympathy and correspondence, a measurement or a form that is in a proportion to the measurements of the cosmos will induce resonance with the spirit and the life force of creation. This force, once conducted, can be utilized either for good or for ill. Through the establishment, the measurement and the laying down of the ley line network and the earth temples, the ancient and the modern geomancer seeks either to enhance the purpose of the divine planetary will, to awaken the intelligence of the planetary being or to divert energy to a personal, corporate or possibly a national purpose. There was no doubt of the enormous power established by the emperor in Peking or the Sun King at Versailles or today, at the Pentagon. But ultimately, power channelled by measurement and alignment based upon sacred proportions will revert to its true global purpose.

It is thus that human intention and activity is capable of interacting with and determining the ley lines and thus the layout and design of the planetary network. In the same manner as the earth's magnetic field already exists the energy of the network exists *a priori*. Yet human intelligence influences and shapes the nature of the lines just as electrical generating stations create local magnetic anomalies. The two are coexistent, mutually affecting each other and may cooperate to each other's benefit.

Ultimately the presence of directed human intention on the lines, on the crossing points, on the temple structures of the planet will awaken the intelligence of the biosphere, the planetary being, and allow the direction of a greater purpose to come into play. To this, our purpose is as a cell in the brain of a greater body. From here we gain a perspective on the role of human activity in establishing the ley line network. We hardly know what we are doing unless we surrender to a purpose greater than that of ourselves, of power stations, of emperors or of nations.

Power Centers

A ley center is where two or more ley lines cross. It may be known as a power center. It appears probable that Sedona is or lies close to a ley center of the planetary network - a place where major planetary lines, or meridians, cross. These planetary leys and their corresponding power centers may be many miles wide so it is not appropriate to say that they cross at exact locations but only in general areas. However, as power centers possess microcosmic centers, wheels within wheels, for our purposes we can define where the greatest energy is concentrated.

It is said that Sedona possesses many major power centers. Page Bryant's classic work has revealed seven main centers which she called vortexes or vortices at the following locations: Bell Rock, Cathedral Rock (Red Rock Crossing), Airport Mesa, Boynton Canyon, the Post Office area and Apache Leap on the Seven Warriors. Indian Gardens was also named but its energy is said to have dissipated. Since then other sites have been felt to qualify as vortices, for example: West Fork, Sunset Point on Schnebly Hill, Coffee Pot Rock and the Chapel of the Holy Cross. Some have gone as far to say that up to 100 sites qualify. At this point there appears to be some confusion as to what a vortex actually is.

Page Bryant made it clear that the nature of vortex energy was magnetic, electrical or a confluence of both. An electrical vortex is stimulating and uplifting. A magnetic vortex works on a more subconscious level, for example for dreams or healing. The vortex of Bell Rock is very electrical. That of Boynton Canyon is a balance of electrical and magnetic forces. Cathedral Rock is more magnetic. The Post Office and Apache Leap are said to be more negative in their affect upon human nature. This system may be directly analogous to the Yin-Yang of Feng-Shui and some aspects of European geomantic practice.

In European geomancy and in some Egyptian and Asiatic systems the principal centers of a sacred landscape may be found to form a chakra system known as a temple. A defined area would contain the seven chakras, corresponding to the energies of the root or base, the sex, the solar plexus, the heart, the throat, the brow and the crown centers. This area may be large or small, applying to a cathedral, a landscape or the whole planet.

Each center or chakra would contain the energy of all seven in varying proportions. Between each of the centers and their inner points would run a multiplicity of ley lines and geometrical systems. If one were to draw them all, the map could become a mass of graphite. Furthermore, the power centers and their interconnecting lines are in a constant state of flux. They become active or passive, dispersing or gathering energy - Ch'i - according to factors ranging from time of day or season, to astrological and weather conditions, to human interaction or ceremonial attunement. The subtle energies of geomancy are rarely still.

A blind spring as defined in Chapter 2 would form the basis for the establishment of a power center, and the name "vortex" would certainly fit its pattern of energies. Although from the description of the power points by Page Bryant what normally comes to mind from the use of the word "vortex" does not necessarily apply to the description of the energies at all.

At such confluences and in suitable circumstances what is known as a "cone of power" may be raised. This is essentially the blending of all the elements in a harmonious energetic form which could then be dispersed for healing on a local or planetary scale or for other purposes. Whether or not this is a vortex is unclear. It is probably true to say that individuals following their intuition will find the location on the energy grid of the area that is most appropriate for them and the prevailing conditions.

A further factor is that ley lines do not necessarily run point to point. This would be in accord with Feng-Shui. They may follow a river system or a mountain ridge or a line of buttes or the gaps in between. Indeed, Sedona may not possess the classic point to point ley system at all due to the irregularity of the landscape, but several examples of possible leys are offered here.

Ley Line A

Due to the large number of buttes, towers, mountains, canyons and other prominent features in the Red Rock Country so many alignments can be found that it would give a straight line ley hunter or a statistician either nightmares or a field day. Ley lines of the straight line variety in the Sedona area therefore need to satisfy extraordinary criteria. Only then may they advance into a realm where the incidence of correlating factors has such a high random improbability that their coincidence becomes a mystery. A line of buttes could not be taken as satisfactory evidence for a ley line if it is part of the same linear geological formation. Yet in terms of Feng-Shui a ridge of buttes could qualify perfectly as a dragon line, as, for example, those above Margs Draw behind Camelhead.

Line A, I feel, satisfies extraordinary criteria. It provides ten sites in as many miles and each site is extremely prominent and correlates to the others in several interesting ways. By standing on the line at point D for example, the Airport Mesa, it is possible to see point A through the saddle in the mountains at C, (see photo on page 31). In itself this is unremarkable but by turning around and looking the other way it is possible to see the phenomenon repeated. The peak at G is visible through the notch in the mountains at F. The relative masses and forms are approximately symmetrical as are the distances involved. There are no other features in the areas of observation which so catch the eye. The line is further enhanced by the low-lying but highly visible, rounded red rock formation known as Sugarloaf at E and by knowing that the Twin Buttes lie on the line at B.

The points beyond the peak at G are not visible from the Airport Mesa. H is one of the Grassy Knolls which are prominent features in the center of the Dry Creek area. I is a red rock pinnacle in Long Canyon known as Isis Rock. It

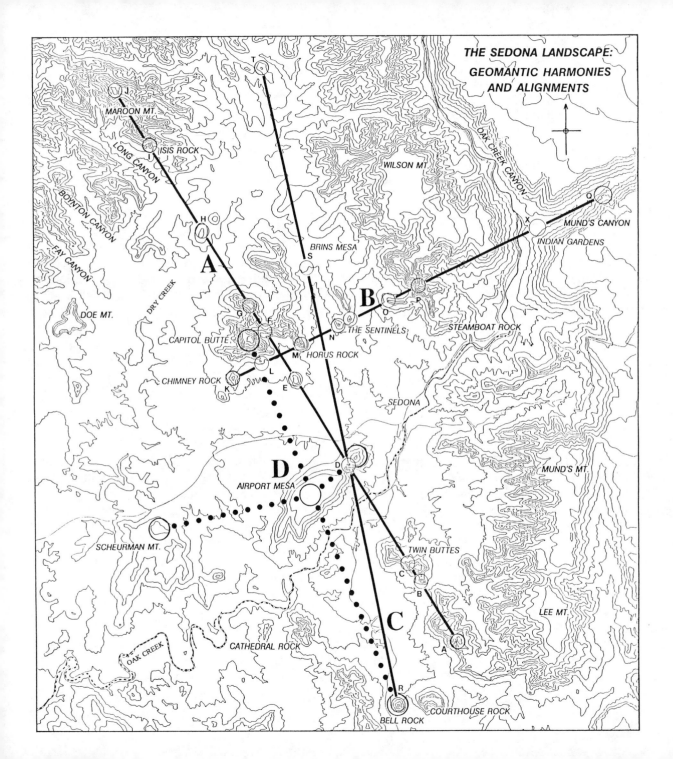

THE SEDONA LANDSCAPE:
GEOMANTIC HARMONIES
AND ALIGNMENTS

stands just before Maroon Mountain at J, the highest point in this area before Secret Mountain and the edge of the Colorado Plateau. In three places the line utilizes a classic feature of all ley hunting - a notch. And it may also extend further, taking in a number of points in Sycamore Canyon, peaks in the west of the San Francisco Range and finally, aligning to the

The Airport Mesa. Alignment A passes between the symmetrical pairs of hills.

Grand Canyon in the area around Havasupai. This line forms the main axis of the sacred geometry and chakra systems given later in this book.

Points G to F equal 1 unit. F to E, A to B and I to J equal 3 units. D to E, C to A, E to G and G to H are all an equal length at 4 units. I to H and D to C equal 5 units. These distances are all within an accuracy of 4 percent.

Ley Line B

This is a very interesting alignment having the possibility of satisfying ley hunters of scientific, astronomical, Chinese or energy divining inclination.

The line, in terms of Feng-Shui, arises in Mund's Canyon. It passes through several rock formations in the area marked Q. Mund's Canyon lies in steep, mountainous

terrain. As the alignment follows the canyon's course it gathers the Yang energy forming a lung mei or a dragon line. Whether the mei continues straight on or follows a sinuous path would be an object of debate or of very difficult divining work given the precipitous nature of the land. The energy of the Blue Dragon passes through Indian Gardens at X, an "old vortex" center before being drawn across Oak Creek Canyon to the rim of the First Bench of Wilson Mountain.

In European geomantic practice it is often demonstrated that it is not always the top of a feature, a hill or its exact center that the ley lines follow but the rim, the edge that is visible from the ground. This also applies to sacred sites such as stone circles where the line glances the edge of the circle at a tangent. The energy, or Ch'i, appears to enter and disperse around the central cone or "vortex," not pass through it.

The next point P, is the gap between the foot of Wilson Mountain and the buttes above Steamboat Rock. The line continues, glancing the edge of the wafer thin red rock ridge at O, before passing between the Sentinels which guard the head of Soldier Pass at N. The line then passes through the notches behind Coffee Pot Rock at M, takes in a buttress of

Old Grayback at L, before terminating at Chimney Rock, K. The last six features are aligned to each other so that from various very inaccessible viewing places, the line just slips through the gaps between the buttes with great precision.

If one prefers a more sinuous path for the dragon the buttes themselves can be taken as anchor points for the line. In this case if alignment were still a criteria the ley would be over 200 feet wide, especially if Coffee Pot Rock were to be included. This would not be without precedent in ley hunting circles where major leys are commonly held to be a mile or more wide. The concept of ley "corridors" is rapidly gaining acceptance. Even small local leys can assume a width of dozens of feet. The width of the line can also vary according to the amount of energy passing through it. A line may be energized for example, according to the phases of the moon.

This line allows for astronomical phenomena to be taken into account. While scrambling around the Sentinels at the time of the Winter Solstice, I observed the sun to set beside Coffee Pot Rock, and upon turning around, to my surprise I saw the full moon rise in the notch below Wilson Mountain. The line may not generate the astronomical potential that a plateau with distant features on the horizon can provide - which is a characteristic of many geomantically integrated sites, the leys becoming "activated" at certain key points in the calendrical cycle of the year - but further research may establish this.

Ley Line C

From the top of Soldier Pass at point S, Bell Rock can be seen sitting squarely between the two small hills of the Airport Mesa, point D. The dragon energy follows the bottom of the canyon and passes between the Sentinels and Coffee Pot Rock. There is a small hillock at point S to mark the line further. From Bell Rock, point R, the notch in the Airport Mesa aligns precisely with foothills at point T before passing on to a notch in the Mogollon Rim beyond. The distances S to T and S to D are equal in length.

A Tibetan Lama was overheard to remark that this alignment linked Sedona with Tibet and further investigation has revealed that if the line were to be extended as a great circle (at 77°49' north of west) then, indeed, it passes through the holy mountain of Tibet, Mount Kailash. A local ley line researcher has said that a total of 19 alignments, one of which goes to Glastonbury, pass through Bell Rock. Whether they were referring to simple alignments or to energy-carrying leys is not clear. In my own experience the maximum number of energy leys passing through a power center has been five, plus one originating or terminating there. This would give a total of eleven alignments.

The Glastonbury alignment at 51°54' north of east is critical to the geomancy of Sedona. It is the mean angle of the main axis of the Airport Mesa and of Oak Creek between Indian Gardens and Cathedral Rock. It is the flight path of the Great Bird. It is also the bearing of the line that runs from Cathedral Rock to Camel Head to Giant's Thumb; and, at Bell Rock itself, that alignment can be observed passing through the saddle at the southern tip of the Seven Warriors and on through to the peaks in the northeast.

At Bell Rock, as at other power centers, the leys pass through the outer rim. The key to the activation of such centers is sound. At the appropriate time and season certain sounds resonating with the rock will induce a spiral of energy to rise in the manner of a snake gathering itself in a coil in order to lift up its head and hiss. Through simple correspondence the rock is linked with the Celtic god Bel. Bel is associated with the color red, with fire, with Mayday, the South, the horned serpent and Glastonbury Tor.

Chapter 4

THE GUARDIANS

Astonishing! Everything is intelligent! Pythagoras.

The Principle of Correspondence

A fundamental premise of geomancy is that of resonance or correspondence. Like resonates with like in the same way as two strings attuned to the same frequency or wavelength will vibrate in sympathy. It is for this reason that architects employ certain canons of proportion in the construction of temples. It is their wish for the structure to resonate in sympathy with the cosmic or the divine ratios. This usage can range from that of a simple circle, to square roots or ratios such as phi - the Golden Section - a proportion which occurs often in the natural world.

A principle of alchemy and magic is that of sympathy. Medicine from owl feathers would heal poor eyesight through simple correspondence; while models made upon the same proportions as the original could be employed to affect the original from afar.

A map is an excellent example of sympathetic magic using a model in geomancy. The contours and the symbols of the map recreate the proportions of the land for the senses. The scale is accurately determined and features can be filled in at will: rivers, vegetation, rocks, buildings and geometrical, anthropomorphic and animistic forms. The same faculties of mind can be brought to bear when examining a map as when standing in the landscape it represents.

Through the principle of correspondence, thoughtforms are drawn to and inspired from features in the landscape with which they resonate. This is especially true if the feature has geomythical harmonies. It is the case that geomantic acts can be performed over a map as well as in the landscape. For the Australian Aborigine there is no difference between the frequencies of the songline being sung and the frequencies of the landscape to which it belongs. The songlines are the living maps of the land. When sung or recounted graphically, as in a painting or a sandstory, they impart the nature of that portion of the earth to the perceiver. Echoes of this can be seen in the Yavapai stories as told by Muukyat and Jim Stacey.

Although it is not possible to say which came first, the landscape or the intelligence of mind, it is this manifestation of the Spirit of the Place - the *genius loci* - which arises out of the interaction of the elemental qualities of the land and the faculties of the human mind, that the ancient traditions were referring to when they spoke of huge river spirits rising up out of their beds, or of giants impressing themselves into the mountains, as well as to finer and subtler objects of resonance. The giants are real. They are embedded in tangible reality. Yet, they take on form (especially anthropomorphic form) through the visionary, symbolic and creative powers of the mind.

Twin Buttes. The Madonna Rock is to the left.

The creation of symbols and of the ancient magical alphabets can be understood in this geomantic context. They assume their power when set in resonance with the properties of the landscape. Many of the original alphabets of the Northern European and Tibetan peoples for example, are known to have had their origin in the trees. The songlines of the Aborigines, the runic script of the druids and the mythical qualities and powers of spirit cannot be separated from the earth. They are one.

A geomantically balanced landscape featuring a temple designed in proportions to resonate with the moon, the sun, a planet or even the zodiac will bring those powers through to the cognition of the beholder, just as a natural feature in the shape of a giant will evoke those qualities. It is only a

culture that has placed the human mind at the center of all things - "I think: therefore I am." - that loses, or has divorced itself from, the power and sanctity of the natural world. Then its sacred sites and the natural glyphs become empty of the spirit power they once contained.

Many of the buttes of the Red Rock Country evoke the qualities of guardianship, of wise and eternal presences watching over the land. There are the examples of the seated figures in the Twin Buttes by the Chapel of the Holy Cross. They are known variously as the Madonna or the Two Nuns, the Apostles or St. Peter and St. Paul. Perhaps all are present if the two adjacent rocks are included. There are the Sentinel Rocks at the head of Soldier Pass where the two buttes display magnificent giants' heads. And there is of course, the bird-being in Coffee Pot or Horus Rock. Yet, for sheer majesty the tall figures enshrined in the central towers of Cathedral Rock stand out above all, and are rightly one of the most frequently depicted sights of Sedona.

The man and the woman standing back to back in Cathedral Rock embody eternal values of humanity: the balancing of male and female, the harmonizing of relationships upon the earth and the essential interdependence of all peoples. These gigantic figures in their sanctified setting form one of the key geomantic signatures of Sedona, and, if their story has not already been told in the legends of the Yavapai, they deserve a myth of their own.

A man and a woman were walking through the land. They just could not get along. The woman always criticized the man's careless ways, his ugly face, his huge penis and untidy clothes. And the man poked fun at the woman's slow walk, her big breasts which she supported with her arms as she ran and her preoccupation with her looks. They were always quarreling and picking at each other. They couldn't have a meal together without some provocation being made.

One day they came to a bright, clear river beside a place of red rocks. They soon found a pleasant place in which to stay. While the woman prepared food and admired herself in the reflection of a pool, the man climbed over the rocks, collected wood and busied himself in building a shelter. He took pride in the deft way he wove grasses together to form a roof. She took pride in the way she ground the corn to its finest texture.

After a while the man grew angry at the woman for not seeing the hard work he was putting into the building of the shelter. The woman grew angry at the man for not coming to eat when the food was ready. "Why don't you appreciate me"? They shouted at each other. "If only you could mend your ways." The sound of their quarreling filled the canyon and the creatures' ears.

They made such a commotion that they woke up the old serpent which lay sleeping in the river's bed. The head of the great snake lifted slowly up out of the river and asked what all the noise was about. Overcoming their astonishment, the man and the woman pointed at each other and both started to talk at once, but the old serpent silenced them by saying:

"When two beings come together they do so in deep respect for each other, whether they are of animal or of humankind. They recognize their dependence upon each other and honor the value of what the other is and does. They also recognize their independence from each other. They understand that they walk their own path and look their own way. For this reason I shall carve a stone where you, the man, and you, the woman, stand back to back to show your connectedness and dependence upon each other and also your independence, your looking your own way. I shall set this stone in a high place of great beauty and sacredness so you shall remember these things forever."

The Central Spires of Cathedral Rock.

The man and the woman were astonished. As the great serpent slid back into the river bed they looked up and saw carved in the stones of the mountain high above them the shape of a man and a woman like them standing back to back just as the serpent had said. From that day on they learned to respect each other. And although they sometimes *had their different opinions they understood that they each walked their own path and no longer criticized and tried to change the other.*

Apart from figures in the rocks with animal or human characteristics evoking qualities directly through similarity - these are called simulacra - there are landscape figures that operate in other forms of sympathetic resonance.

The Giants

For many peoples the landscape features are described in terms of the forms or the actions of the ancestors. A common myth shared all over the world is that once the land was inhabited by a race of giants. See for example the Arizona myth told by Hiram Hodge on page 19. Or the stories of the Titans and Cyclops in ancient Greece. While in Britain giants were held responsible for the placing of many erratic boulders whose origin otherwise appeared incomprehensible, or for the building of megalithic monuments such as Stonehenge.

Giants could be described as elemental presences, energy fields created by nature rather than by man and then given anthropomorphic qualities. They do not necessarily have to have human form. An archetypal presence underlying a variety of tree, a plant or other elemental form can easily take on human characteristics that are far larger than life due to their ubiquitousness.

At the same time, places can retain a memory of what has been felt or enacted there. It may be that in a sensitive state we can perceive an image or a sound encoded in an "earth-field" of what happened there in the past. It is known that some crystalline rocks, especially quartz, can store patterns of energy as electrostatic charge. Thus, not only can the ancient past be known from an ability to read the encoded place-memories, but fields of energy can be created or reinforced by the continuation of similar actions or thoughts or the retelling of myths at a particular place.

The theory of giants I would like to pursue here is one in which the pattern of the total landscape can be described in terms of the form of a being, human or animal, viewed from either horizontal or vertical perspectives.

One immediately evident example in the Sedona area is the skyline of Courthouse Rock. From the north the butte forms the silhouette of the head of an Indian warrior who lies with his chin to the east and the top of his head to the west. There is a story that treasure lies in his mouth. I do not know where this story originates and it may not refer to literal treasure. And then there is the Yavapai legend of Skata-kaamcha spreading himself over and into the landscape.

A stunning and complex example of recumbent landscape figures is provided by the Glastonbury Zodiac in Somerset, England. Found by author Katherine Maltwood in the 1920's it appears that nature and the human hand conspired to create in the outline of hills, rivers, woods, fields, roads, earthworks and buildings the pattern of a huge terrestrial zodiac. That is, the star map of the twelve zodiacal constellations fits features provided by a landscape some 33 miles in circumference and 11 miles in diameter.

Each figure of the zodiac lies in its respective place. In several instances they differ from the form of the figures as we now know them. The figures correspond to an earlier form of the zodiac used by the Chaldeans. Scorpio for example, is an eagle, not a scorpion. Cancer is a ship and not a crab. Capricorn is a single-horned quadruped and not a fish-tailed goat. And Aquarius is a phoenix; not a water carrier. In each case, however, there are intimate associations with the meanings of the signs as universally known.

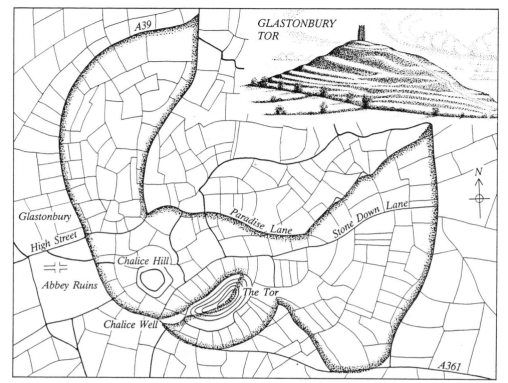

The figure of Aquarius in the Glastonbury landscape. The pattern of lines is formed by field boundaries which approximately follow the contours. Roads delineate the outline of the wings. The head is formed by the landmark of Glastonbury Tor. At one time the figure was almost entirely surrounded by water. This was the mythical Isle of Avalon. The creation of the Zodiac has been a continuous process embracing all ages down to the present day. It is as though an invisible blueprint has been followed by nature and the human hand alike.

For example, the watery characteristics of Aquarius are provided by the phoenix being located on the former island of Avalon (Glastonbury) and by the fact that springs gush out from the place that marks the location of its beak.

It is also significant that Aquarius in this landscape zodiac assumes the form of the mythological phoenix, a bird said to be consumed by fire and to arise from its own ashes. It appears that a similar radical transformation is required before we can advance into the age ruled by the constellation of Aquarius. Meditation on the other transformed zodiacal symbols also gives interesting results. These giant figures of the Glastonbury Zodiac - Sagittarius for example, is over 5 miles long - form a terrestrial temple whose corres-

pondence to the stellar pattern in our galaxy, the Milky Way, generates a resonance that enhances the awareness of all who live within or are conscious of it. As a resonant temple structure it serves the geomantic purpose of at once being a transmitter to and a receiver from the stars. It stretches the human imagination considering that the best viewing place of the whole zodiac is from a point about 5 miles up.

The pre-historic peoples of Britain appeared most aware of the zodiacal form in the natural landscape and labored to enhance it with earthworks. They were working for a vision that could not be appreciated fully from any place on the ground. The head of the Aquarian Phoenix, located on Glastonbury Tor, gives the best view one can expect.

From the study of natural and human enhanced giant figures in the land the question arises easily, can we find such figures in the Sedona landscape?

37

Chapter 5

FLORA AND FAUNA

What is this joy? That no animal
falters, but knows what it must do?
Those who were sacred have remained so....
Denise Levertov. From the poem
"Come Into Animal Presence".

The Trees and Plants

In the same way as it has not been my intention to describe the geological formation of the Red Rock Country, such information being readily available in all the guide books, so only the briefest mention will be made of the plant life in the area. Not that the rocks and the vegetation are of any less significance to geomancy - they are fundamental to it. However, rather than focus on many details only the briefest outline will be given. It is sometimes true that knowing the names and the nature of things down to the finest detail can be a distraction from their intrinsic relationship to the whole of which they are a part. Naming a thing becomes a substitute for knowledge. Once categorized it can be distanced, exploited or tucked away on a museum shelf. This is a result of the spirit-matter separation that has long characterized Western thought.

Knowledge of the properties of vegetation was essential for well-being and survival for peoples with a long relationship of dependency upon a landscape. Their practical uses, their medicinal and nutritional values were known. This information was organized into a ritual system of correspondence with the calendar, the deities, the minerals, the animals and so on. Each plant taking its appropriate station in the system. The Celtic Tree Calendar for example, formed a highly developed cosmology which children learned in such a way that through reference to it the properties of any plant could be understood by its structural relationship to the whole. We may be certain that the native peoples of Arizona developed such a system, perhaps integrating it around the medicine wheel teachings.

In essence, the predominant plants in the Red Rock Country are the evergreen trees: ponderosa pine along the rims of the high canyons, below them the evergreen oak; Arizona cypress at the mouths and the bottoms of the canyons; and almost everywhere the juniper and pinyon pine. These tree communities cloak the land in green. They cling to apparently impossible rootholds and provide the basis for other plant and animal life.

The next most eye-catching plants are the cacti, the prickly pear, the yucca (Spanish bayonet), and the agave (mescal). These last two were essential to the life of the desert dwellers for food and for fiber. Other shrubs include

Horus Rock.

the red-barked manzanita, the mesquite, catclaw acacia, chaparral and silktassel bush, all easily identifiable. All these plants exhibit characteristics that are a part of the hot, dry ecology of the desert. They are sharp, low-growing, fibrous and evergreen. Only along the edges of the creeks do the taller, softer deciduous plants grow. These include cottonwood, sycamore, box elder, willows, herbs and berries.

The variety of plant life is surprisingly rich and deserves to be maintained. As in the rest of Arizona the greatest threat to vegetation is from cattle and erosion. Rain, when it falls, is heavy and runs off taking the top soil with it. Plants stabilize the soil. However, they would do better if simple measures such as building with minimum disturbance of trees and simple contouring practices were adopted. Sedona could become self-reliant in food. The soil is rich. Besides the obvious beauty, this was the reason the settlers came here in the first place. Local gardens supplied the market in Flagstaff since Sedona enjoyed many more frost free days than did Flagstaff located above the Mogollon Rim.

The Birds and Animals

When Antonio de Espejo entered the Verde Valley in 1583 he listed parrots among the birds he saw. It is hard to know quite what he meant by this as parrots certainly do not live in Arizona now, unless he was referring to tame birds or feathers brought into the area through trade with the south. The migratory route of the Hopi Parrot Clan is said to be northwards indicating a southern origin and the Yavapai include the parrot in their myths. Espejo also mentioned other creatures which are still to be found around Sedona, though in depleted numbers.

The black bear, once extremely common in the area is now restricted to remote areas such as Bear Sign and Secret Canyons, as is the mountain lion. Although threatened, the antelope and the migratory herds of elk manage to hold their own. However, the grizzly bear and the jaguar have completely disappeared. The Wapiti deer and the beaver are rapidly going the same way.

Although hawks are still very common - especially Cooper's and Red-tailed Hawks - the Golden Eagle is seen less and less. The Bald Eagle is now reduced to only 23 known mating pairs in the whole of Arizona. Jackrabbits, squirrels, chipmunks, skunks, coyotes, javelinas (wild pigs), lizards, various snakes - especially the Gopher and Western Garter snakes - doves, swifts, Great Blue herons, hummingbirds, flickers, mockingbirds, wrens, woodpeckers, ravens, chickadees, jays, owls and many other birds are all commonly found in the canyons.

As is well known from biological studies, the animals dwelling in an area form a delicate pattern of interdependency between themselves and their habitat. Their presence contributes to the total set of harmonics that forms the resonant structure of a place. If one note is omitted from the song then that place is weakened geomantically. Instead of presenting to the senses a full and varied experience of the life forces it presents an impoverished one. The contrast between a rich ecosphere and a dull one is quickly realized when one visits a natural area of woodland and then a plantation of a single variety of trees. In the latter the birds do not sing, the undergrowth does not rustle with life and the streams flow listlessly.

The animal signatures of a place are fundamental to its geomancy. The naming of a place after a creature may signify its predominant intrinsic quality. Bear Sign Canyon, Rattlesnake Canyon, Doe Mountain, Wild Horse Mesa, Beaver Creek and Grasshopper Flat are all places where this quality has been recognized.

At the top of Soldier Pass is Brins Mesa named after Old Brin, a bull who once ranged freely in that area. He proved impossible to catch and was shot by two cowboys who failed to bring him down with their lassoes. A second resourceful animal was a mare called Marg who would abscond after every shoeing, knowing that it meant a long trip for her. She would take refuge in the area below Mund's Mountain which being entirely enclosed meant her recapture was inevitable. The area was named Margs Draw in her honor. These two examples do not form a part of the natural co-evolution of the biosphere in the region. Nevertheless the stories express something about the qualities of the places the animals chose as their refuge and are examples of myths in the making.

The Power Animals

In the traditional and ancient cultures of the world animals play the role of mediator between the different varieties of human experience and between the human and other worlds. Knowledge could be attained through the process of transformation or metamorphosis into the spirits and the skins of the animals. Transition through the various rites of passage was thus facilitated.

Among the Hopi, individuals belonged to the clan of a certain Kachina who walked a particular migratory path and possessed specific legends. This Kachina, often in an animal form, would be their ally and help them in their lives. In the shamanistic traditions the animal allies would assist the shamans in their work. This usually involved a transformational journey into other realms of being.

The animals are agents of this process because they are instinctively at one with the condition of their bodies and that of the earth around them. They provide a vocabulary that is both symbolic and real. It is made up of tangible actions, things and expressions rather than of abstract sets of ideas. The power animals provide a way of speaking about things in which spirit and matter are implicitly seen as one.

Personal power animals allow us to attune to the feelings, needs and wisdom of our own being. They bring us to ourselves. Many human activities serve as distractions which take us away from ourselves. Humans will often do anything to prevent feeling, even driving the body to the point of exhaustion with activity or inertness with drugs. We try to transcend or resist our own life force, something an animal will never do.

The power animals allow us to share in the full range of earthly experience. Soaring with the bird gives us its vision and ease of movement. The fish teach us how to negotiate deep currents. The deer show us how to run. The bear and the mountain lion show us strength and ways of facing our fears. The otter's acute hearing teaches us how to listen. Through them we can dissolve the boundaries of self and move from a limited to a greater perspective.

Giant's Thumb or The Owl.

In many cultures this world-creating and immanent sacredness of the animals was honored by geomantic acts in which the animal spirit was set in resonance with the landscape. The songlines or the spirit paths of the Australian Aborigines were walked and sung by the ancestors in world-shaping dreamtime. Among the ancestors were the animals - lizard dreaming lines, dingo dreamings, wallaby billabongs - all were places where the ancestor emerged, walked and went "back in." A person whose dreaming was wallaby would know the songs and the nature and the power of the landscape where the wallaby ancestors' story lay. At certain times they would go to the dreaming sites and perform ritual to increase the power of the place.

In the Americas many huge figures lie in the landscape: from the spiders, monkeys and birds of the stony highlands of Peru to the Serpent Mound in Ohio. In Britain horses hundreds of feet high were carved on the green hillsides. And in all of Europe cave paintings over 20,000 years old show the wild creatures in all their glory.

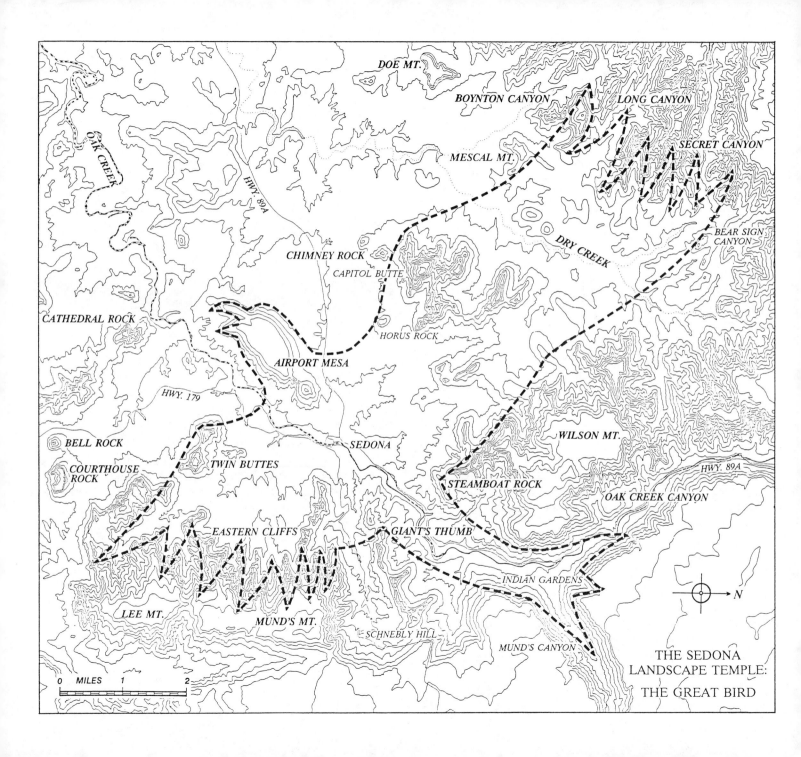

DOE MT.

BOYNTON CANYON

LONG CANYON

SECRET CANYON

MESCAL MT.

OAK CREEK

HWY. 89A

BEAR SIGN CANYON

CHIMNEY ROCK

CAPITOL BUTTE

DRY CREEK

HORUS ROCK

CATHEDRAL ROCK

AIRPORT MESA

HWY. 179

WILSON MT.

HWY. 89A

BELL ROCK

SEDONA

STEAMBOAT ROCK

OAK CREEK CANYON

COURTHOUSE ROCK

TWIN BUTTES

EASTERN CLIFFS

GIANT'S THUMB

INDIAN GARDENS

N

LEE MT.

MUND'S MT.

SCHNEBLY HILL

MUND'S CANYON

0   MILES   1   2

THE SEDONA
LANDSCAPE TEMPLE:

THE GREAT BIRD

The relationship between the land of Sedona and the spirits of the Sinagua and possibly the ancestral Hopi clans has been forgotten. It might be reconstructed from study of the remaining rock art: petroglyphs (carvings) and pictographs (paintings). Snake pictographs in Hartwell Canyon, Long Canyon, Secret Canyon and Red Canyon do make the presence of a snake clan seem a possibility. However, the fact that someone has drawn a snake does not necessarily mean they are members of a snake clan. What would really clinch the evidence would be the finding in the area of the central and the six radiating shrines that form the traditional geomantic configuration of the Hopi Snake Clan.

The Eastern Cliffs forming the wingtips of the Bird.

There is also the originating legend of the Yavapai which included the presence of the bird in the hollow log which carried Komwidapokuwia. Exactly how this is related to the landscape where the log came to rest has become obscured by the dispersal of the culture. Yet there are obvious bird symbols in the natural landscape: Coffee Pot Rock resembles a powerfully beaked bird, Steamboat Rock resembles a huge bird lifting itself up, head and wings outstretched over the land and Giant's Thumb from some southern viewpoints resembles an owl perched on the rocks with folded wings.

And if Oak Creek Canyon and Mund's Canyon are seen as the forked tail feathers of the bird, then the body of a giant bird lies on Sedona. One wing terminates in the canyons of the Eastern Cliffs below Mund's and Lee Mountains. The other wing lifts into the canyons beyond Dry Creek, while the head of the bird is made up of the Airport Mesa even down to the details of the beak.

The bird swoops toward the southwest, toward the place of the emergence of many of the migratory paths of the clans, and away from the Hopi lands and the home of the Kachinas, the San Francisco Peaks. Oak Creek flows through the length of its body. It is conceivable that the ridges running east from Sedona which include Mantle Rock, Teapot Rock and the Giant's Thumb around Schnebly Hill form the legs and feet of the bird.

There is no necessity to prove the existence or non-existence of this bird. It exists in the geomantic imagination and will be set in motion in the landscape of the collective mind only to the extent that it takes hold as an idea. It may thus be a bird of the future birthing itself now, rather than a bird of ancient legend. Whatever else it represents, it is oddly appropriate that airplanes landing and taking off from the airport align themselves with the path of the bird and aim for its head.

Chapter 6

GEOMETRIC LANDSCAPE TEMPLES

*There is only one temple in the world
and that is the human body.*
Novalis. "Pollen and Fragments" 1798.

*Man has no Body distinct from his Soul for that call'd
Body is a portion of Soul discern'd by the five Senses.*
William Blake. "The Marriage of Heaven and Hell" 1793.

Patterns of growth

Research into atomic, molecular and cellular growth has shown that a common pattern can be demonstrated in many of the varieties of form found in the natural world. It is known that silicon atoms, the elemental substance from which quartz is made, bond together via the single free electron of each atom in a spiral form. A quartz crystal is a visible demonstration of the pattern of bonding of the basic atomic building blocks. It can be shown to have had either a right or a left-handed spiral in its history of growth.

The breakthrough into understanding the structure of the DNA molecule - and therefore the processes of biological reproduction and growth - was reached when it was realized that the molecular chains of the DNA bonded and separated in a spiral form known as the double helix.

In nature many forms can be seen to follow patterns of expansion on which spirals can be drawn: the placing of leaf buds around the stem, the horns of rams and deer, pine cones, cacti, shells, seed pods and the proportions of the human body all follow this pattern. In our bodies the relationship of the length of our forearms to the distance from our wrists to the first knuckle, and so on to the second and third knuckles and to the fingertips can be shown to proceed in a relationship of 1 to 1.61818 or phi.

The phi proportion, otherwise known as the Golden Section or the Golden Mean, underlies the spiral pattern of growth in nature. It can be expressed mathematically in the sequence of numbers attributed to the Italian mathematician Fibonacci. In this sequence two initial terms are added together to form the third term.

$$1.1.2.3.5.8.13.21.34.55.89.144.$$

Any two successive terms in the series will be in approximate relationship to each other as phi.

$$8/5 = 1.6 \quad 55/34 = 1.6176 \quad 144/89 = 1.6179$$

As Theodore Schwenk demonstrated in his beautiful book *Sensitive Chaos* the movement of the spiral is present in the free-flowing forms of nature. Water flows in spirals in ocean waves, in rivers and from dripping taps alike. This pattern also emerges in the movement of masses of air. When musical notes were played on a violin, a single coil of smoke varied its spiral pattern as the air molecules vibrated with the sound. As a result of these experiments, Schwenk posed the question, to what music do the great bodies of water and of air, and for that matter of wood and minerals, dance as they unfold their spiral forms?

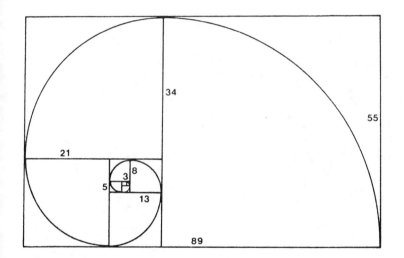

This spiral pattern of expansion based upon the Golden Section or the relation of 1 to 1.61818 is to be found in many of the forms of nature. It is present in the nautilus shell, in the arrangement of seeds around the head of the sunflower and in the proportions of the human body. Where these ratios occur, resonance with the natural patterns of growth and regeneration insures harmony and accord with the universal will. For this reason geomancers, architects and artists employed this canon of proportion in the construction of temples and works of art.

The Pentagram

One of the properties of the pentagram is that the lines bisect each other according to the Golden Section. The relation of AB to BC is that of 1 to 1.61818 or phi. By its presence in the pentagram, the Golden Section signals that where 5's are found in the pattern of the natural world conditions will be most beneficial to life, as for example in the number of petals in the flowers of the edible plants.

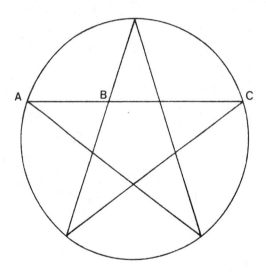

In geomantic practice the number 5 in the form of the pentagram or the pentagon often occurs in architecture and in landscape temples. For example, it is present in the massive pentagram found in the placing of the Cathar shrines and temples which lie in the landscape of the Rennes le Chateau region in the south of France. There it is associated with the mysteries of Mother Mary and the Holy Grail. The diagram on the following page shows a pentagram emerging from out of the natural features of the Sedona landscape.

45

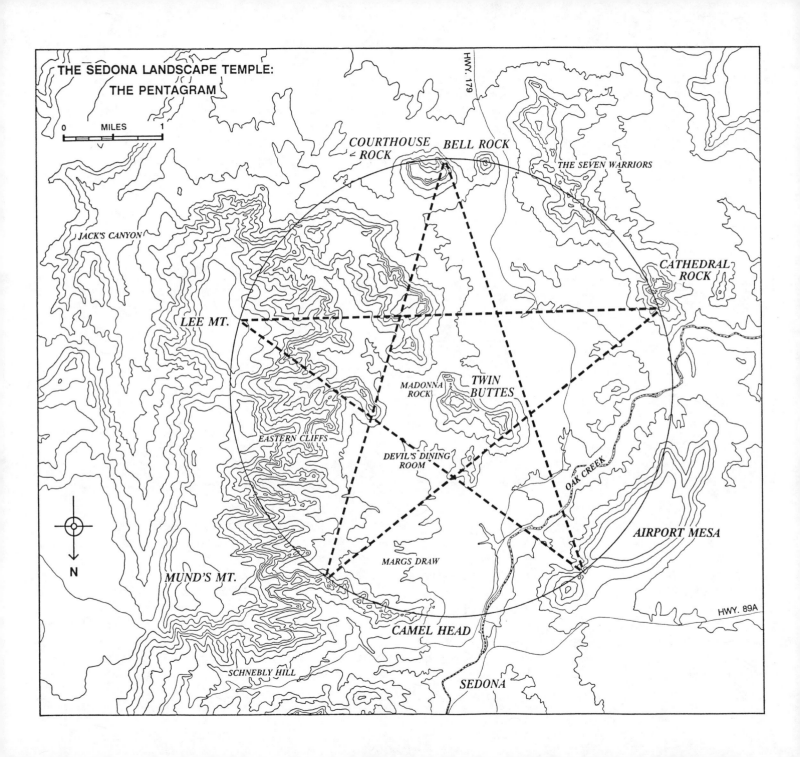

The points of the pentagram lie on Courthouse Rock, Cathedral Rock, the small hills by the Airport Mesa known as the Airport Vortex, on one of the buttes in the row behind Camel Head at the foot of Mund's Mountain and the last point on the summit of Lee Mountain. The center of the pentagram falls on the rock known as the Madonna beside the Twin Buttes.

It is also of interest to note that Bell Rock, the Airport Mesa, several peaks of The Seven Warriors (Apache Leap), the line of buttes behind Camel Head and several buttes and peaks of Mund's Mountain lie on the circumference of the circle formed by the pentagram. Other prominent features in the area lie on lines defined by the arms of the pentagram or by additional lines drawn through the center point to the five points of the star.

It appears that the figure, through its ability to integrate so finely with the predominant features of the area, can assume an existence beyond one of mere random chance. The statistical improbability of it correlating to the placement of equivalent natural features elsewhere is of an extremely high order.

The points on the summit of Lee Mountain and on the line of buttes behind Camel Head are not specific. They cover large areas and so create a degree of imprecision for the generation of the pentagram. But the three points on Cathedral Rock, Courthouse Rock and the Airport Mesa create an exact spatial order which will divide a circle into five equal segments by themselves and are sites of major interest. Furthermore, Lee Mountain should not be ignored. As a feature it lies on a major fault and is the highest point to the south in the Sedona area. As for Camel Head, the antediluvian people in the Verde Valley hunted that creature to its extinction in North America. Only the name and the head in the rock remains.

According to many ancient traditions "Man is the measure of all things," and the ideal human proportions lie in the canon defined by the Golden Section or phi. If the full height of the body is taken as 1, then the distance from the navel to the top of the head is equal to $1/phi^2$, and the distance from the navel to the feet is equal to $1/phi$. The relationship with phi also appears when the human body is placed in the pentagram. The head and limbs reach out to the points, the sexual organs lie in the center.

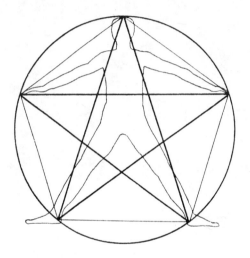

"Man," however, is not all things. Humanity takes its place in a vast and beautiful creation. It depends on our estimation of the value that we give to this creation that defines our relationship to it.

The area defined by the Sedona pentagram could be said to be the Temple of the Law of Human Life on Earth. By placing the human body in the figure the right foot rests on human law as represented by Courthouse Rock and the right hand rests on the balance of male and female as represented by Cathedral Rock. From the west the central

The buttes behind Camel Head. The point of the Pentagram is to the right.

and the natural worlds. Looking at the pentagram as a whole it could be said that human law and the right relationship of male and female are balanced by a recognition of the natural law and the interdependency and right relationship with the animals.

The naturally formed pentagram in the Sedona landscape shows that we are "the measure of all things" only in that we are a part of all things. We are not separate from them, nor are they in any way worth less and thus able to be freely exploited. The manifestation of the pentagram in the landscape itself is a test of how much we are willing to credit nature with intelligence and consciousness.

If the Twin Buttes, which correspond to the sexual glands, were seen as the mythical Komwidapokuwia, the bird who accompanied her and her grandson Skataka-amcha, the postdiluvian world of the Yavapai and Apache could be geomantically conceived of as emerging from the center of the pentagram, the symbol of human life and regeneration. It is curious that the Sedona Memorial Grounds are located where the heart of the human figure would be and that Madonna or "Great Mother" associations are present in the immediate area. There is an especially beautiful bronze sculpture of mother and child beside the road near Poco Diablo.

spires of Cathedral Rock appear as an enormous hand with fingers raised in the gesture of a priest's blessing.

The figure could lie in other ways but my own intuition is that it lies as suggested. For then the opening to the spirit world falls between the two small hills in the Airport Mesa which is said to be one of the major vortices of the Sedona area and is referred to by many as the "hub." The remaining limbs of the human figure rest on the Eastern Cliffs which culminate above Sedona in Camel Head, in the wild valleys running up to Lee Mountain and in the area known as Margs Draw, where the mare Marg took refuge.

The left hand side of the figure in the pentagram signifies to my mind the dependence of humanity on the animal

The Pentagram and the phi formula it contains is a proportion not a numerical term. It yields a progression that is continuously evolving. The outer manifestation is in a constant proportion to the inner pattern, as nature continually reproduces herself yet evolves from the original form.

From the natural world as expressed by the pentagram and the number 5, for example the 5 perceptual thresholds of sight, touch, taste, smell and hearing, and the 5 limbs of the body and the sets of 5 fingers and toes, we can now move to further dimensions of the divine order as represented by geometric configurations in the Sedona landscape.

The Hexagram

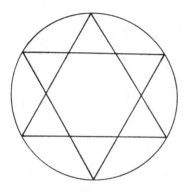

In numerology the number 1 represents unity or a point; the number 2 represents duality, multiplicity or a line; and the number 3 is representative of the trinity, a plane, the emergence of form in a dimensional world which the principles of a point or a line cannot reveal. The number 4 represents materialization into form, the world, nature and the square; number 5 is the evolving principle of the natural world, finding its expression in the human form and the pentagram; and the number 6 is the leap, 3 + 3, into a multi-dimensional world which the principles of a square or a pentagram cannot reveal.

Around the winter solstice in 1988, I was sure that somewhere in the Dry Creek area I would find something corresponding to a 6. One day I walked up Soldier Pass, around the tall buttes to the north of Old Grayback and climbed up onto the rocks by Devil's Bridge to obtain a good view of the landscape. I had no idea what to look for. All I knew was I had an intuition that somewhere in the area lay a 6, whatever that was.

The features that stood out most powerfully in the rock formations as I walked up Soldier Pass were the buttes below Wilson Mountain to the east and Lost Wilson Mountain. Around the corner into the Dry Creek area were the Grassy Knolls, Doe Mountain and the high peaks beside Secret, Long and Boynton Canyons. In the distance were the Cockscomb, and of course, Old Grayback to the south. I could make no particular order out of the rock formations. Returning home I learned that the Dry Creek area was once densely populated by the Sinagua whom the Hopi include among their ancestors.

I wondered if the six I was seeking related to the geomantic configuration described by White Bear in *Book of the Hopi* as the shrines of the Snake Clan. The six shrines were said to be placed in an equidistant spatial order around the central emergence mound and kiva of the Snake Clan. I felt it would be hard work scrambling over the rocks to find and map the most likely candidates for shrines among the Indian ruins. There are plenty in the area but I did not know what to look for.

However, I took out the maps and placed a compass on the point above Devil's Bridge where I had been drawn to sit. I found that practically all the prominent features I had noted fell on a circumference that they shared in common with the point of the pentagram touching the Airport Mesa. Moreover, four of the features - Doe Mountain, the prominent tower above Long Canyon before Maroon Mountain, Lost Wilson Mountain and the center of the line of buttes just below Wilson Mountain and just above Steamboat Rock - lay

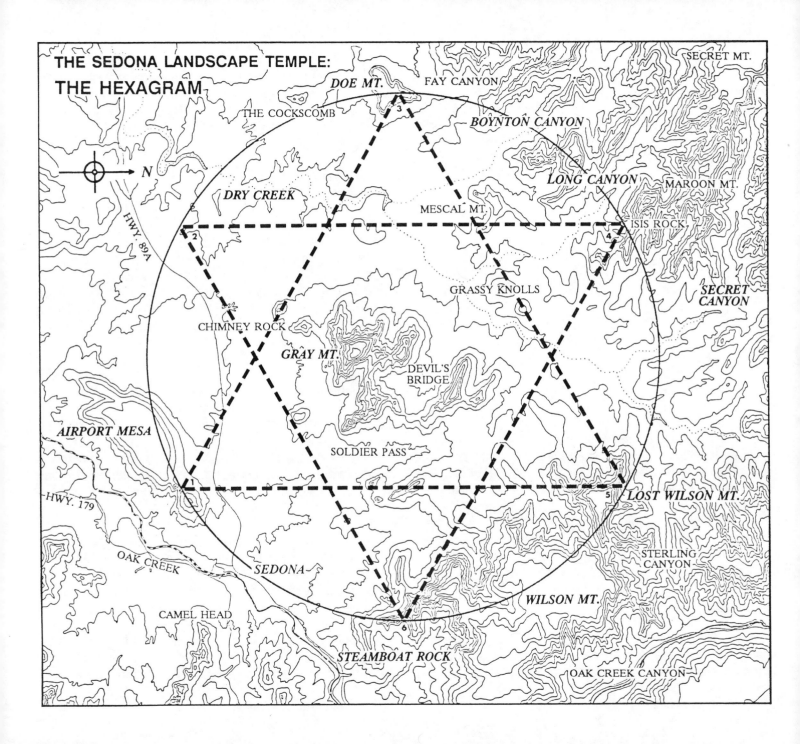

THE SEDONA LANDSCAPE TEMPLE:
THE HEXAGRAM

SECRET MT.

DOE MT. FAY CANYON

THE COCKSCOMB

BOYNTON CANYON

DRY CREEK

LONG CANYON MAROON MT.

MESCAL MT. ISIS ROCK

N

HWY. 89A

SECRET CANYON

GRASSY KNOLLS

CHIMNEY ROCK

GRAY MT.

DEVIL'S BRIDGE

AIRPORT MESA

SOLDIER PASS

LOST WILSON MT.

HWY. 179

STERLING CANYON

OAK CREEK

SEDONA

CAMEL HEAD

WILSON MT.

STEAMBOAT ROCK

OAK CREEK CANYON

on the circumference of the circle in such a way, that along with the Airport Mesa and an indeterminate point to the southwest very near the garbage dump, they divided the circle into six equal parts. I had my 6, the hexagram or a six-pointed star, made up of two intersecting triangles!

I noticed that many other prominent features in the area fell on the lines formed by the geometry of the hexagram and circle, showing that once again the goodness of fit went way above statistical probability for random placing. Lines, for example, drawn from point to point of the hexagram include features omitted from the outline of the star. The east-west line passes through buttes in the Soldier Pass area. The northeast-southwest line passes through the peaks to the north of Old Grayback, while Thunder Mountain as a whole appears to lie symmetrically in the center hexagon.

But the real excitement came when I realized that the hexagram shared common centers and common points with the pentagram when a line was drawn through the two figures. Other landscape features also fell on the line, such as one of the Grassy Knolls, the Sugarloaf just below Coffee Pot Rock and points beyond. This confirmed that I had not only a good ley line (described as line A in Chapter 3) but I also had a connection between the two circles of 5 and 6 in the Sedona landscape.

By way of observation the two figures relate to each other in a proportion of the square root of 2, which means the area of the hexagram is exactly twice that of the pentagram. More on this in the following chapters. They share lines that are close to true north-south and east-west. Both have at their centers buttes that dominate their respective areas - Capitol Butte and those by the Chapel of the Holy Cross - and they align to each other through their common shared point, the hub or the gap in the Airport Mesa.

To return to the principles of numerology the 6 is the number of wisdom adopted by King Solomon as his seal in the form of a star. The interpenetration of two 3's in the form of triangles signifies the meeting of the 6 directions, all the knowable dimensions, the heavenly and the material worlds beyond which the mundane human perceptual faculties cannot ordinarily reach. Yet implicitly contained within the hexagram is the threshold to the supra-dimensional worlds. This is the 7 which is represented within the hexagram by the central point - at once the limit of ordinary perception and the gateway to the beyond.

The central point of the hexagram lies on the great peak of Supai and Coconino sandstone to the south of Devil's Bridge. The secluded and beautiful canyon below contains Indian ruins in a good state of preservation. The Devil's Bridge is an arch in the red Supai formation formed by weathering. The name may indicate a place of great natural power. In lands where transcendentally oriented cultures have overlaid earlier earth oriented cultures, the name "devil" is frequently applied to shrines or centers of chthonic (earth-arising) power.

It has been intuitively suggested that the arch be known as Rainbow Bridge. This would be appropriate for the seventh or center point of a six-pointed star, since the visible spectrum is made up of seven major colors. One other natural bridge, Fay Canyon Arch, lies on the circumference of the circle on the north side of Fay Canyon.

Whether or not the Hopi ancestral people established the seven shrines of the Snake Clan in the Red Rock Country is unclear. There are Indian ruins on Doe Mountain, on Steamboat Rock, beside Lost Wilson Mountain and in Long Canyon, all of which fall near the points of the hexagram, as well as there being the ruins near the center of the figure. We also know from the pictographs that the Sinagua were

Thunder Mountain from the northeast. Devil's Bridge lies on the right hand side of the distant valley. The peak above it forms the centerpoint of the Hexagram. The Grassy Knolls are in the foreground.

time. In Aboriginal culture the twin serpents of creation are known as the Rainbow Serpents of the Earth and of the Sky - the descending and ascending dimensions. The synthesis is to be found in the interpenetration of the two triangles of the hexagram.

Second, the Sipapu or emergence place of the Snake Kachina of Hopi ancestry is a hole in a mound of earth. The Devil's Bridge or Rainbow Bridge is a possible candidate for this place of emergence. The name Devil is frequently applied to the chthonic serpent. Furthermore, six serpents are often shown together in Mesoamerican symbology. They are to be found at the four corners of many pyramids with two descending from the top of the pyramid to the bottom. They are said to represent the six directions.

Third, in world mythologies the serpent is associated with wisdom, the symbol for which is the six-pointed star. The seal of Solomon, proverbial for his wisdom, was the six-pointed star.

Fourth, in the natural world it is the five which most often demonstrates the proportions of plants beneficial to humanity; for example, the five petals of the flowers of the fruit-bearing trees. It is the six and seven petaled plants which demonstrate less beneficial qualities; for example the poppy and the leaves of the potato. The poisonous quality of many snakes links them to the numerology of the six.

Fifth, the serpent is associated with the mysterious energy of the kundalini. In Hindu cosmology this energy is said to lie coiled in the root chakra at the base of the spine.

using symbols like those used by the Hopi Snake Clan today. These can be seen in Hartwell Canyon (above Boynton Canyon), Long Canyon, Secret Canyon and in Red Canyon (Palakti). It would take further research to advance this hypothesis. At present there is only subjective information to go on.

First, the intuitive renaming of Devil's Bridge to Rainbow Bridge allows a connection to be made with universal serpent mythology. The number 7, the 7 colors of the rainbow and the 7 steps of the pyramid are associated with the feathered serpent Quetzalcoatl or Kulkulcan of Mesoamerican culture, who is prophesied to rise again at this

When the serpent energy rises and ascends through the chakras with their associated rainbow colors, it eventually enters and opens the seventh or crown chakra. Through the threshold of the opened crown chakra a further set of radiant chakras - said by some to number six - comes into play. This opened seventh chakra is symbolized by a feathered serpent in some traditions and a horned serpent in others. The latter is common in the pictographs of the Northern Arizona Indians. (See page 89.)

In the Celtic Tradition the initiates into the higher mysteries were entitled to wear a torque - a snakelike necklace coiled in high tension. They would be depicted with horns or holding a serpent with a ram's head. These symbolized their ability to access their inner powers. In the Hopi tradition the horned members of the Antelope Clan dance with the Snake Clan at the Snake Dance. To further the connection between the snake and the hexagram a description of each point now follows.

Cliff Dwelling in Long Canyon.

Point 1. The Hub or the Airport Mesa.

This is the tip of the downward descending triangle. It is the point where spirit fully engages with the human world like a stone sinking into the depths of water. It is where the hexagram joins with the pentagram along their common axis. This is described in Chapter 3 as Ley Line A. It could be called "The Gateway to Heaven." There are several medicine wheels in the vicinity which honor the six directions through their horizontal and vertical axes. One wheel, now broken up, on the summit of the conical hill may be extremely old, though I do not have the archaeological knowledge to say how old. From here all points of the pentagram and four points of the hexagram can be seen. This is the dynamic point of balance. Do not be alarmed by the planes taking off overhead. Easily accessible.

Point 2. The Garbage Dump.

Strictly speaking, the compactor site. This is one of the base points of the ascending triangle, the place where human actions can be read through what has been discarded. Any archaeologist will tell you, paradise is when you find the trash heap. It has a negative polarity and is a place of great teaching, especially for us of a consumer culture when what we have jettisoned now threatens the entire earth. Approach with caution, glass is scattered everywhere.

Point 3. Doe Mountain.

This is one of the points which form the base of the descending triangle. This conspicuous and naturally fortified mesa is climbable from the south (very steep) and the north (not so steep). It is table-topped due to its cap of hard stone. It has a positive polarity and was intuited to be a place concerned with the higher forms of animal life. There are many Indian ruins in the area, including an amphitheater on one of the benches of Fay Canyon where the Indians were said to gather in council.

Point 4. Isis Rock.

This is the apex of the ascending triangle, the point where matter becomes fully spirit. Situated on the north wall of Long Canyon below the most prominent tower formation on this part of the Mogollon Rim, Isis Rock can be seen from many points along the trail into the canyon. The rock, some 200 feet tall and quite separate from the cliff face, is divided into three columns. The two outside columns form arms with hands lifted to the temples in a gesture of inner realization. Some say the butte standing behind with a conical hat resembling a spiral is Isis Rock. Here, as in Boynton Canyon and the Twin Buttes, the many forms of the goddess make the ancient legends of her presence in the Sedona area come alive. There are snake pictographs nearby. Relatively accessible.

Point 5. Lost Wilson Mountain.

This is the second point of the base of the descending triangle. It has a negative polarity. Wilson Mountain was named after a hunter who died at the claws of a grizzly bear. Lost Wilson Mountain presumably refers to it being a peak detached from the main body of the mountain. It would be extremely arduous to attempt to climb this peak and would require equipment and skill. Many UFO's have reportedly been seen in this area; but as a place of spirit it is probably best left alone.

Point 6. Above Thunderbird Rock.

The second point on the base of the ascending triangle. It is a place of tremendous concentration of positively polarized energies. Buttes align themselves to it from all directions. The energy field is so large that it is hard to say exactly where the center lies. There are several ways to enter the area, the best being up Jordan Road and then taking trails to the east (before the Sheriff's Shooting Range!). The energies lift and revitalize, even shock. This is perhaps best expressed by Thunderbird Rock (Steamboat Rock) to the south. The Indian ruins here are not accessible except to those suitably equipped. Since it is unlikely that they were dwellings, they may have constituted some form of ceremonial or initiatory structure.

The combined geometry of the pentagram and hexagram may be briefly contemplated at this point. The pentagram signifies the temple of the body while the hexagram signifies the temple of the spirit. The whole joins together through the awakening and the rising of the serpent power along the common line of intersection of the geometrical figures. The serpent energy then penetrates through to and opens the door to the supra-dimensional world symbolized by the number 7 at the center of the hexagram. (The number 8 signifies the fullness and the infinite nature of the universe. The number 9 represents completion, purification and the step beyond. 10 is new beginnings.)

Geomythically, the combination of the two geometrical figures corresponds to the legends of Komwidapokuwia and Skatakaamcha. Komwidapokuwia and the bird, after emerging from the first world and regenerating the people as

Long Canyon. Standing in the center of the picture, Isis Rock forms the topmost point of the Hexagram and looks back down the central Dragon Line of the Sedona Landscape Temple.

symbolized by the pentagram, pass on to become deities in the spirit world symbolized by the hexagram. Hence the stories of an old woman spirit presence in the canyons of the Dry Creek area. While, at the same time the legends of her grandson, Skatakaamcha, allow us to conceive of his body as lying along the axis of the entire system.

The combined figures reveal through their geomantic qualities - geometrical, numerological, symbolic and mythical - that the Sedona landscape forms a temple of the highest order. The qualities of the landscape establish a resonance with the celestial realms making it a place where humans can come to open to their higher selves.

Chapter 7

THE SACRED GEOMETRY OF SEDONA

Geo - metry: *the measure of the earth.*

Measurement

In Geomantic practice the use of measurement is of vital importance. Through measurements that are in a ratio to the terrestrial and the heavenly orders temple structures achieve cosmic harmony. The fundamental units of measure which have been universally recognized as resonating with the cosmos are those which are based upon the movement of the heavenly bodies and are proportionately related to the axis and the circumference of the earth.

For the practical purpose of navigation the nautical mile was established as one minute of one degree of the earth's circumference (60 x 360). From satellite observations we know the earth's meridian circumference to be 24,883.2 miles. This figure divided by 360 degrees gives a measure of 69.12 miles for 1 degree. Divided by 60 minutes gives a measure of 6,082.56 feet for 1 nautical mile. The earth however, bulges slightly at the equator giving a circumference of 24,902.95 miles and thus a longer nautical mile of 6,087.38 feet. Such considerations need to enter into the calculations of navigators.

As an example of this measurement in ancient geomancy, estimates of the length of the base perimeter of the Great Pyramid have been 3,041.28 feet, exactly half the shorter nautical mile, and thus half a minute of the earth's meridian circumference. It would seem the ancient Egyptians knew the exact circumference of the earth, a fact unknown until Newton's time, and divided the circle by 360 degrees and each degree into 60 minutes.

One second of one minute (60 x 60 x 360 degrees) of the earth's circumference is equal to 101.376 feet, which is exactly 100 Greek feet. This shows the Greeks were also extremely accurate in their establishment of the meridian circumference of the earth.

100 Greek feet are equal to one second of the earth's circumference. 60 seconds or 1 minute equals 6000 Greek feet or 1.2 Greek miles. 60 minutes or 1 degree equals 72 Greek miles and this multiplied by 360 gives the earth's circumference as 25,920 Greek miles. This number, 25,920, is the number of years the sun takes to pass through the zodiac. So to establish this number as the measure of the circumference of the earth furthers the synchronicity between the heavenly and the terrestrial ratios.

It would appear the ancient world derived its numerology from the movement of the stars. Those other ancient astronomers, the Mayans, also derived their measure - Hunab - from the movement - Ku - of the heavenly bodies, and built their temples and complex pyramids in harmonic proportions to those time scales.

The English mile and foot also show a relationship to the cosmic ratios. If the earth's equatorial circumference of 24,902.95 miles is divided by 360, the resultant measurement of 365,243 feet is equivalent to the 365.242 days in one year. Incidentally, the meter was intended to be a proportion of the earth's circumference but was based upon an inaccurate measurement. This observation and the source of many of the measures given come from the excellent work of John Michell.

To return to the pentagram and hexagram of Sedona, the unit of 101.376 feet, or 1 second of 1 minute of 1 degree of the earth's circumference, is the measurement that recurs constantly.

The diameter of the pentagram is 101.376 feet x 220 = 22,302.7 feet, or 1 part in 5,890 of the earth's circumference. The diameter of the hexagram is 101.376 feet x 311 = 31,527.9 feet or 1 part in 4,167 of the earth's circumference. The distance of the two figures combined is 101.376 feet x 531 = 53,830.7 feet, or 1 part in 2,440 of the earth's meridian circumference. In other words, exactly 2,440 Sedona Landscape Temples laid end to end would go completely around the world.

The diameters of the Sedona Landscape pentagram and hexagram relate to each other in the proportion of the square root of 2. This means that the square formed by the diameter of the circle of the pentagram has a diagonal that is equal to the diameter of the circle of the hexagram. This is a relationship of 1 to 1.4142 or $\sqrt{2}$. Which means that the area of the circle of the hexagram is exactly twice that of the area of the circle of the pentagram. Root 2 is the number that multiplied by itself yields 2. So, if you had to solve the problem of doubling the size of a square or a circle the answer would be to either lengthen the sides or the diameter by the factor of 1.4142.

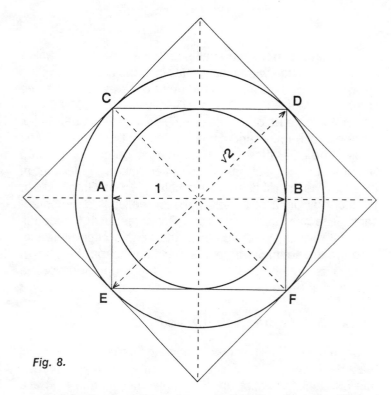

Fig. 8.

In this diagram it can be seen that the diameter (AB) of the circle of the pentagram forms a square (CDEF) whose diagonal (DE) is equal to the diameter of the circle of the hexagram. If AB is 1 then DE is 1.4142 or $\sqrt{2}$. As the tone of a string can be doubled by halving its length, so halving a square through its diagonal creates the side of a square whose area is double in size. This can be realized through counting the triangles of the squares of each circle.

Through $\sqrt{2}$ the area of the circles and their squares increases or decreases by a factor of 2. $\sqrt{2}$ therefore expresses the power of multiplicity toward unlimited expansion or contraction. In the words of the geometrician Robert Lawlor "the extreme, essential polarity of the universe, unity and multiplicity, is perfectly represented and observable in the simple drawing of the square and its diagonal."

Later in this book we shall see that in the Basic Chakra System contained within the pentagram, the diameters of the crown, third eye, throat and the heart chakras are the same at 101.376 feet x 20. This is 2,027.52 feet or 2,000 Greek feet or 20 seconds of circumference or .4 of 1 part of 25,920, the zodiacal number and circumference of the earth in Greek miles. The solar plexus is twice that diameter, being 4,000 Greek feet or 40 seconds of circumference or .8 of 1 part of 25,920. The sacral chakra's diameter is 1,000 Greek feet or 10 seconds or .2 of 25,920 parts of the earth's circumference. The base chakra's 10,000 Greek feet or 100 seconds is equal to 2 of 25,920 parts of the earth's circumference. Through these measurements the Landscape Temple of Sedona is harmoniously related to the proportions of the heavenly and the terrestrial spheres.

Alchemy and the Squaring of the Circle

In alchemy and sacred geometry there is a magical practice known as the "squaring of the circle." This has been described as the ability to construct a square whose perimeter is equal to the circumference of a circle or whose areas are the same. Various architectural structures around the world have attempted to address this question through the geometrical ratios of their construction.

The Great Pyramid solves this problem by the fact that the circumference of a circle drawn by using its height as the radius of the circle is equal to the perimeter of the base of the pyramid. The Sedona Landscape Temple offers a new solution to this practice. This is vital to the resolution of the unmanifest, unified, irrational and unquantifiable properties of the circle with the manifest, multiple, rational and quantifiable properties of the square.

The two circles of the landscape temple represent the qualities of earth and of spirit. The pentagram's circle repre-

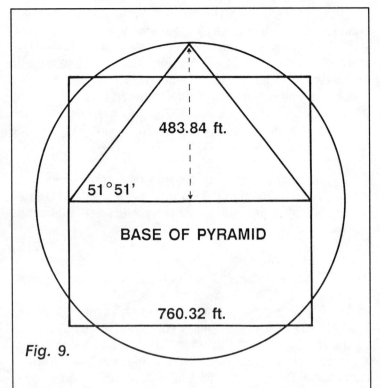

Fig. 9.

The Great Pyramid's solution to the squaring of the circle. If the perimeter of the base is taken as 3,041.28 feet and the height as 483.84 feet, this height when used as a radius creates a circle of circumference 3,041.22 feet. (483.84 x 2 x pi, taking pi as 22 divided by 7).

This checks out if other measures of the pyramid are used, e.g., 3,024 feet and 481 feet. The figures are disputed, but most authorities agree on the 51 degree 51 minute slope of the pyramid's sides.

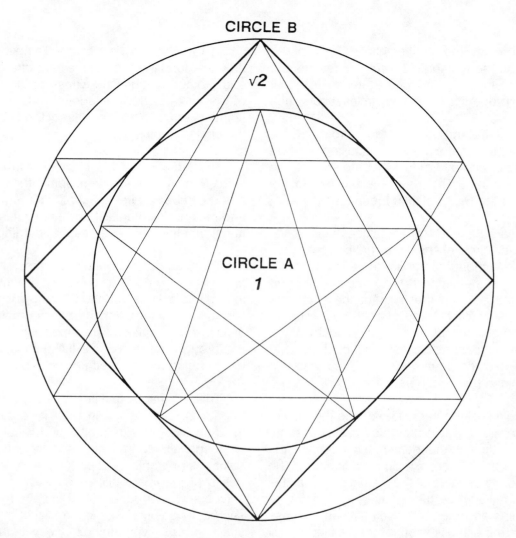

CIRCLE B

√2

CIRCLE A
1

Fig. 10.

The Sedona Landscape Temple's solution to the squaring of the circle. In this diagram the diameter of Circle A enclosing the pentagram is given a value of 1. The diameter creates a square whose area is also 1 (1 x 1) and whose diagonal is √2. Circle B, enclosing the hexagram, has a diameter of √2, while a square drawn around it would have an area of 2 (√2 x √2). Therefore, Circle A is in the same relationship to Circle B as their two squares which is 1:2. Half of Circle B is equal to the area of Circle A.

The hexagram has a further relationship to Circle A in that its component triangle's base lines intersect the midpoints of the lines of the square of Circle A; and that the distance between the hexagram's points is equal to half √2.

sents the sphere of earth, the undifferentiated base of the manifest world, while the hexagram's circle represents the sphere of spirit, the unified quality of the unmanifest spirit world. How are the properties of the two circles reconciled?

The circles are related through the square root of 2, by the ability to derive one from the other by enclosing or being enclosed by a square, and by the fact that the area of one is twice that of the other. The square is the key to the relationship between the two circles in the landscape.

Without the square the circle of earth does not evolve. Without the square the circle of spirit does not progress from unity to multiplicity. Without the square there is no resolution of the principle of matter with the principle of spirit. Alternatively, it could be said that without the circle the square of the manifest, multiple forms of earth would find no rest, no unity and no qualities of spirit. The geometry of the Sedona Landscape Temple reveals that it is the relationship between the circle and the square that is critical and this relationship is obtained through the square root of 2.

The circle of matter, of the human body and the natural world develops when its energy is grounded in the construction of the square. This is the fundamental sacred act. It is the establishment of the vertical axis and the finding of the four directions. It is the building of the temple on earth. It is simultaneously the building of the earthly body, the sanctified temple structures and the earth itself. When all these are related through the establishment of the center, the six directions and the sacred canons of proportion and measure, the vision of divine harmony between the earth and the cosmos is achieved. It is precisely these sacred acts that were performed by Hanyiko' (Frog), the first shaman of the Yavapai, at the beginning of the first world. In the shade of the tree he had set up he gave the people the calendar and the names of all living things.

In the Sedona Landscape Temple when a square is drawn around the circle of the pentagram, the circle of earth, and a diagonal obtained whose proportion to the diameter of the circle of the pentagram is the square root of 2, its length is equal to the diameter of the circle of the hexagram, the circle of spirit.

The squaring of the circle of earth - the Pentagram - leads directly to the circle of spirit - the Hexagram - which in turn could be squared to lead on through the dance of unity and multiplicity, manifest and unmanifest form, to ever new transformations of being, each emerging from the other.

The practical interpretation of these abstract geometrical principles may be as follows: the grounding of one's vision in tangible actions and the building of the Temple on Earth allows the manifestation of Spirit and quickens the evolution of all living organisms. The implications of this are profound for through the actions of living beings on the earth the divine being makes itself known.

This is a teaching of immanence, of responsibility and of hope. Of immanence in that, it places the sacred back inside the self, inside matter and within every living thing. Of responsibility in that, as there are no transcendental solutions to problems of our own making - not in an afterlife nor in divine intervention - we have to reap what we ourselves sow. Of hope in that, inspired by the sense of the sacred inside ourselves and realizing our individual responsibility to all living things, we will move forward more strongly than ever to further the building of the New Jerusalem, the heavenly Temple on Earth.

Through the square, the circles of earth and spirit touch. Through the Landscape Temple of Sedona a new solution and meaning is offered to the enigmatic, alchemical concept of "the squaring of the circle."

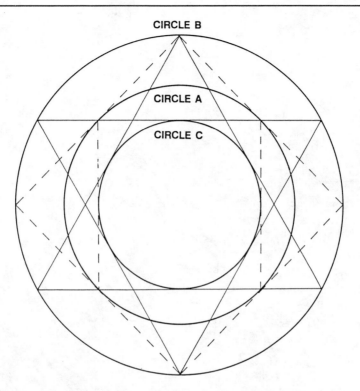

CIRCLE B

CIRCLE A

CIRCLE C

Fig. 11.

When Circle A is enclosed by a square (side = 1, diagonal = $\sqrt{2}$) and a hexagram (distance between points = half $\sqrt{2}$) inscribed within the circle (B) of that square, the lines of the hexagram subtend an inner circle (C) and square whose relationship to Circle A is the same as Circle A's relationship to Circle B (C:A::A:B), that is, $\sqrt{2}$. Unlike the pentagram, the ratios of the hexagram relate to spirit, to the circle and the square root which governs its expansion. The ability of the hexagram to subtend within itself a circle (C) via the circle (A) of the pentagram, reveals a further mystery expressed in the alchemical saying "as above, so below."

If the figure is taken as a map of the cosmos, with Circle A representing the surface of the earth then the sixfold symmetry of the hexagram represents the heavens above and the world below. The 6 is present not only in the qualities of spirit but also in the hexagonal structure of the bulk of the crystals which form the mantle of the earth. Once again, through the location of a pentagram in a circle relating to a circle containing a hexagram in a ratio of the square root of 2, the naturally formed Sedona Landscape Temple reveals a mystery equal to that encoded in the temples of the ancient world.

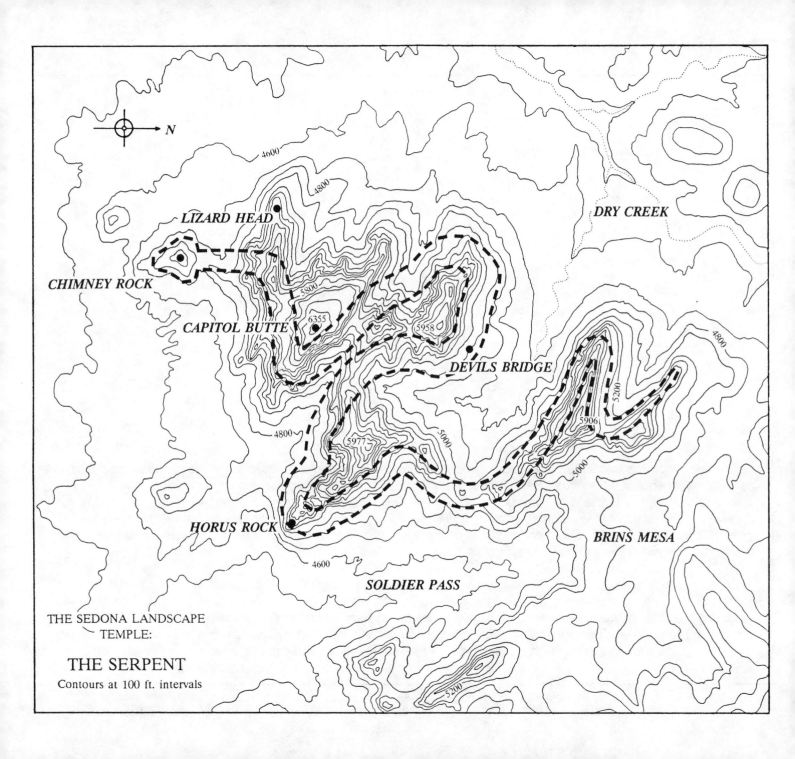

N

4600

4800

LIZARD HEAD

DRY CREEK

CHIMNEY ROCK

5800

CAPITOL BUTTE

6355

5958

DEVILS BRIDGE

5200

5906

4800

4800

5000

5977

5000

HORUS ROCK

BRINS MESA

4600

SOLDIER PASS

THE SEDONA LANDSCAPE
TEMPLE:

THE SERPENT

Contours at 100 ft. intervals

5200

Chapter 8

THE SERPENT

The act of union between the earth and the heavens is necessary for the continuation of life; for if there is no lightning, the earth becomes barren. In order that plants should grow, it is necessary to fuse the electrical currents of the atmosphere with the streams of terrestrial energy.   John Michell. "The New View Over Atlantis" 1983.

The Landscape Serpent

Continuing my pursuit of the snake in the Dry Creek and Thunder Mountain area, I was struck by the serpentine arrangement of the range of peaks that formed Thunder Mountain itself. The 4,800 foot contour delineates a discrete mountainous area with Chimney Rock and Old Grayback to the south, Horus or Coffee Pot Rock to the east, while the whole mass follows a sinuous path to the north terminating near the top of Soldier Pass.

From my original vantage point above Devil's Bridge or Rainbow Bridge, I had noticed how the red rock strata on the opposite, north wall of the canyon formed long, snaking benches which girdled the peaks. The dragon energy or the lung mei of Feng-Shui could be seen approximately following the 5,000-5,200 foot contours at this point.

Some months later, after the discovery of the landscape hexagram and its connection with serpent mythology through numerology, Hopi lore and other landscape features, I returned to this earlier observation of the benches and followed the path of the movement so created around the remainder of the mountain. To my delight I found that

the pattern of Thunder Mountain formed a serpent. As can be seen from the maps (see also the map containing the hexagram on page 50) the serpent winds its way around the peaks of the mountain embracing each one in turn.

The tail of the serpent lies on the northernmost point of the mountain, runs along the edge of the long slender peak, then snakes around the benches of Rainbow Bridge Canyon on down to Horus Rock. There, the path of the serpent makes a sharp turn back and is swept upwards and over the notch just to the east of Old Grayback through which the central ley line of the Sedona Landscape Temple passes.

The point in the anatomy of a serpent where the heart is located falls between the peak which forms the center of the hexagram and Rainbow or Devil's Bridge. We have already seen how this point has serpent associations so it comes as no great surprise to find it forming a vital organ in the body of the landscape serpent.

Above Devil's Bridge is a bench in the red rock which carries the serpent's energy around the central peak of the hexagram, and rising out of the vegetation there is an unusual rock formation. Said by some to be heart-shaped, or cobra-headed by others, the rock has passages for eyes which look toward the east and allow the serpent current to pass through.

The serpent then moves around the head of the formation that lies at the center of the hexagram, and, being unable to turn back upon itself, rises with the mass of Old Grayback. At this point the serpent is lifting its neck if not to the full 6,355 feet of Grayback then to the 5,800-6,000 foot contours. The head then, in the manner characteristic of snakes, drops downward to terminate on the ridge which runs westward from Grayback. On the end of this rests the feature known as Lizard Head. In the *Book of the Hopi* there is an extremely close connection between the Snake and Lizard Clans, so here is another example of geomantic resonance at work.

Chimney Rock is a further feature to the south of Lizard Head. It can be conceived of as lying in the path of the serpent current to form a head more in keeping with the overall size of the serpent. Its horizontal outline is an ex-

Lizard Head from the south. This and Chimney Rock offer alternative heads for the Landscape Serpent.

cellent approximation of a snake's head and it has been suggested that Chimney Rock itself forms its horns.

It is also possible to conceive of the neck of the serpent spiralling around Grayback, perhaps making a complete turn before coming to rest on Chimney Rock or Lizard Head.

It is up to interested individuals to intuit or divine the path of the serpent for themselves. I was unable to do as much groundwork as I would have liked due to the extremely precipitous nature of the terrain. It is possible to climb all these peaks but only with adequate protection, clothing, water and extreme care due to the tendency of the yellow Coconino sandstone to slide. In fact, it is dangerous; people have required assistance for their descent.

I was able to climb the peak just short of 6,000 feet that lies at the center of the hexagram and was rewarded with spectacular views all around. The circular basin which cradles Thunder Mountain could be appreciated in its entirety and the points of the hexagram on the surrounding higher ground were very distinct. Also, for the first time, I was able to see much of the length of the dragon line which runs through the Sedona Landscape Temple as presented in this book and fully appreciate the synchronicity of its alignment. I could even see the Rainbow Bridge almost directly below.

On the center peak's summit I felt on the threshold of a new kind of knowing. I sensed a strong vertical axis. This, coupled with the six surrounding points on the horizontal plane, gave the impression of being in a precisely defined matrix such as that of a double terminated quartz crystal.

It was easy to feel at the focal point of a vast antenna and for a moment I understood how the body of the earth with its iron, crystalline and mineral core receives and transmits the electrical and magnetic waves which fill the universe. The earth's crystals share a universal atomic structure which allows them to resonate with and so receive the imprint from the extraterrestrial bodies: planets, suns, galaxies and other energy sources. In turn they generate a powerful electromagnetic field in which we live and which extends many thousands of miles out into space.

On the thin layer of the earth's surface I was a point midway between its core and the surrounding electromagnetic fields, which I realized I could not have perceived were it not for the crystalline nature of matter and its organizing power which gave me life.

It is hard to explain, but I felt the creative, universal matrix was to be found in the play between the center of our earth and the galactic center and beyond to the center of the galaxy which the Mayans call Hunab Ku. I was in the middle, and appreciating this scheme of things, for it dispelled any hierarchical notion of the rocks or the earth being "below" us in any scale of life. I recalled the alchemical adage "the way up is the same as the way down," and was immediately back with the serpent. For in dragon lore the attributes of the creature are exactly that of being able to move between earth and sky. It lives under the earth guarding untold gem and mineral wealth and with its wings is able to fly up to heaven. In oriental art the dragon is frequently shown dancing with an orb representing the sun.

From this point of vision I could not come back down to earth for I had never left it. There I was, still on the top of the mountain, with the manzanita, the view and the turkey vultures riding on the air currents all around.

Thunder and Lightning

I will not recap here the full connection between the serpent and the number 6 and the landscape hexagram, but a glance at the maps will show the integrity of the association among the features. The rock formations which make up the serpent are evenly placed in the center of the hexagram to form a very satisfyingly balanced arrangement, while the serpent itself moves in a direction that it shares in common with the Great Bird. If the serpent were to be extended, its length would be found to be roughly equivalent to the diameter of the circle in which the hexagram lies.

To return to the geomantic configuration of the Hopi Snake Clan - that is, its central shrine being surrounded by 6 spatially equidistant ones - is it possible to find from the evidence of the landscape serpent further proof that the Hopi ancestors passed through the Sedona area in their migrations and employed the form of the hexagram in their honoring of the Snake Kachina?

The answer still has to be no. The landscape serpent is equivocal, subjective information and will remain so until objective, probably archaeological evidence can be found. But I would like to leave this for your contemplation. The ancient, native name for the range of peaks which includes

The Heart of the Serpent.

Old Grayback is Thunder Mountain. And one of the ceremonies it is the duty of the Hopi Snake Clan to perform is that of rainmaking in the summer season. To break the hold of the hot, dry months of midsummer the Hopi Snake Clan and Antelope Clan perform the Snake Dance with live snakes which are said, among other things, to attract the thunder and the lightning and thus bring the rains. See for example, the description of this ceremony in the *Book of the Hopi*.

At the same time, the association of the serpent, the name Thunder Mountain and my own personal experience of there being a bridge between earth and sky, is vividly illustrated by the lightning flash which moves in a serpentine path. And, to return full circle to the intuitive renaming of Devil's Bridge as Rainbow Bridge, we find not only the Australian Aboriginal tradition of the Rainbow Serpent of Earth and Sky being linked through the thunder and lightning, but also the Native American legend of Rainbow

Bridge being the pathway between the worlds. And finally, in the Yavapai legends it is through the means of the lightning flash that Skatakaamcha returns to earth after visiting his fathers:

"From the heaven to the earth went two lines of Dark Medicine lightning from Sun and two lines of thunder lightning from Cloud. All together they make four. Skatakaamcha floated down the four lines of lightning to earth. There he knelt and, pressing his hands on the earth, sank into it singing as in this song... In his right hand he had Dark Medicine. In his left hand he held Rain Lightning."

In this way, through geomantic investigation of the Sedona landscape, we find confirmation of the reasons why this land was held to be sacred. The clues hidden in the land, in the remaining ancient names and the intuitively given names, in the legends preserved by native tradition and in the geometrical and animistic forms, all combine to enhance our understanding of this Sacred Earth.

The Moving Earth

It was pointed out to me by a long term resident of Sedona that the serpent may be very disturbed. Snakes being creatures with long, vulnerable vertebrae fear being trod upon by heavy animals like us. Many of the rattlesnakes, for example, the banded rock and the ridge-nosed varieties, pose no threat to people, but we pose an enormous threat to them. She said that the Apache war paint was a "don't tread on me" mimic of the facial stripes of the ridge-nosed rattlesnake.

Sedona is undergoing considerable construction work, and although some is in keeping with the natural beauty, much includes destructive activities such as tree stripping, blasting and filling. A hill was removed from the area beside

Hwy 89A to the south of Chimney Rock in the summer of 1989 to make way for a supermarket. A considerable amount of dynamite was used. A new hill was made from the rubble nearby. Such actions from a snake's point of view would pose an enormous threat to its vulnerable vertebrae. It would seem to the landscape serpent that the heavy footsteps of men were getting closer.

It may be that my inability to divine the path of the serpent in the area of Old Grayback is due to a fundamental dislocation of its energies. It may be drawing back. We must therefore be extremely careful, for it is when a snake is threatened that it coils itself in order to strike.

The human race, nature and the mineral worlds can live in peaceful and cooperative existence but only when human actions and objectives contribute to beneficial conditions for all. If the earth is seen in terms of a model of interacting systems and one system is out of balance, it might be a while, but it would eventually happen that negative, or positive, feedback from the other systems would bring the wayward system - in this case, the human - back into equilibrium.

There is a story from Australia that a mountainous ridge was the dwelling place of a serpent dreamtime ancestor that had buried many of its yellow eggs there. When the ridge was proposed as a suitable site for the extraction of yellow earth (uranium) the local Aborigines were horrified. They said the dreaming of this serpent included the instructions that the eggs should never be disturbed. If they were, then the eggs would break open and nothing would stop the entire surface of the earth being consumed by maggots.

Closer to home, thanks go to Mike Harrison and John Williams, Yavapai from Fort McDowell, for telling us of spirits - Kakaka - still around in the hills:

Kakaka are just like Indians, but little tiny people. Maybe 3 or 4 feet high. They live in the mountains, Four Peak, Red Mountain, Superstition, Granite Mountain near Prescott. We call Granite Mountain "Wikute". They can get in and out of the mountain. They are just like the wind, like air. You can hear them hollering at night and sometimes some people can see them. The Kakaka never die. They were around this country before the people. They were the first in this country here. All the tribes know about the Little People. The Kachina of the Hopi, that's the same ones.

The Kakaka are still around in the mountains. They are always there helping us. They also live down here in Fort McDowell among us. They have many houses... And we never build houses at such places. Never use these places for anything. These are sacred places. They keep watching over us all the time.

At this time of human existence upon the earth, our technological abilities far exceed our wisdom. Through using these abilities to serve unprecedented material growth the forces of desire know no limit. It may well be that through remembering our common time of arising with all other beings on the planet and honoring the trees, the plants, the animals, the rivers, the rocks themselves and the wisdom of the tribal peoples, we will bring ourselves back into balance, back into the equilibrium, before we are driven off the earth.

Through geomancy we may reawaken to our true power. For its practice is tangible; what we do and what we build has immediate effect upon the world. At the same time it is a magical practice; for it teaches that every act, thought, measure and form, however abstract, resonates with everything else. Geomancy may empower us through the knowing that everything we think and everything we do can serve the well-being of all life on earth.

Chapter 9

THE TEMPLE CHAKRA SYSTEM

Skatakaamcha said to people in the Red Rock Country:
You open me down the middle from my head to my crotch,
And turn me belly down upon the ground,
Then sing around by body
And you will get my songs.
If you sing my songs you will keep alive.
Muukyat.

Part I - The Basic System

An extremely important aspect of the Sedona Landscape Temple as presented in this book is that of it being composed of several centers which correspond to the sevenfold Chakra System.

In Chapter 3 the idea of a discrete area of the landscape containing the seven vital centers or chakras was given. It was said that the area could be of any size and that these centers were often incorporated into the form of many sacred sites from the cathedrals of medieval Europe to the temples of ancient Egypt. What was not really made clear was how the form of the sevenfold temple related to the seven chakras of the human body.

The ancient temples were built according to precise geometrical and aesthetic formulas to achieve certain effects upon the physical, emotional, mental and spiritual bodies of the visitor or pilgrim. The combination of light, sound, texture, aroma, shape and movement as the visitor passed through the temple structure was calculated to stimulate the vital centers so as to balance, cleanse and open the energy bodies and induce a "peak experience." The Gothic cathedrals, for example, were so arranged that the base chakra formed the entrance at the western end, the main crossing formed the heart while the crown chakra usually lay in a Lady Chapel at the eastern end.

The question to be asked of the Sedona Landscape Temple is whether it, as a natural temple rather than a man-made one, can open the chakra system of the visitor, and if so, how can this be achieved?

It is my opinion that the Sedona landscape possesses in natural abundance all that was carefully crafted into the ancient temples of the world. It is for this reason that the native peoples of the area called this land sacred and developed mythologies around it which transformed the natural landscape into a potent and symbolic place.

It may be said that rock formations like those of Sedona were possibly the original inspiration to create temples in the centers of human habitation. The effect of the rhythmic patterns caused by wind and water on the faces of the rock was observed and repeated in the movement of the architrave, nave and pillar in the temple. When examined closely it may have been seen how the crystalline structure of stone played its part in creating the shape of natural formations and this geometry was then imitated in architecture. The hexagonal columns of basalt that can best be seen crowning the rim of Oak Creek Canyon, and the structure of quartz - which is present in a highly evolved form on Wilson Mountain - provided the original inspiration for the pattern and the design of the temple. Clearly this cannot be taken too far, for organic forms such as the animal or the human body would have also played their part.

The effect of color would not have been overlooked either. Where colors are dull, inspiration is low and feelings flat and lifeless. Recent medical studies have shown the importance of light entering the eye for physical well-being; and the stimulating effects of the spectrum of color have been utilized by artists in a wide range of media from stained glass windows to high-tech light displays.

Anyone who has experienced the rainbow of colors that Sedona provides - the reds, yellows, whites, blacks and purples of the stone, the blues and greens of the vegetation, the scintillating effect of the clear sky, the abundant sunshine and sparkling water - will know this is a place where inspiration, well-being and the sense of the numinous thrive.

On a walk one day to the center of the pentagram, a local architect, Max Licher, spoke of how the sounds of nature are maintained throughout day and night to provide each place with its essential note or signature. Though the sources of sound vary, the essential note remains the same.

The early birds would sing at dawn to be taken over by the wind in the trees created by the warming sun. The sound of water might be constant, or the night insects might alternate with those of the day. The canyons would focus or funnel sound so that each place would resonate in a specific way even though the sound source, for example the call of a raven, would remain the same.

Sound may play a larger role in ecological equilibrium than is immediately apparent. The sound or vibratory rate of air frequencies sustain a pattern with which plants and animals, and humans, if they are sensitive enough, instinctively harmonize. An animal might not only know that this was "home" but exactly the appropriate place or time of day or season for a particular activity from the sound frequency around it. Considerable confusion could arise in species dependent upon certain sounds if the signature of each place was unbalanced by audio pollution: the constant buzzing of traffic, helicopters, airplanes or inappropriate human activity.

Everything that has been said here about sound may apply equally to aroma, which is a whole field in itself.

The study of place-sound signatures may have formed the basis for the building of temples with certain acoustic properties. It would have been noticed that particular places in nature had specific effects and these could be duplicated in structures where they could be controlled and amplified. From the wish to produce certain sounds, the measurement of walls, doors and ceilings may have arisen and the ratios or canons of proportion arrived at.

We know for example, that the note A vibrates at 440 cycles per second. This is a wavelength that can be directly translated into ratios of measurement. These measurements may also be related to the frequencies of color. Of course, sound can be used to create either disharmony or harmony and from simple beginnings in caves or canyons the science of music and its effects has evolved.

I can think of no better example of the sound properties of the Sedona landscape than that which has been one of the main sources of material in this book, the harp and voice of the Sedona musician Anne Williams. Through her ability to attune to the essential elemental or place-sound signature of an area of the landscape I was able to establish this geomantic interpretation of the Sedona Landscape Temple. Her 15 year residence and deep understanding and knowledge of the land enabled me to research and write this book in a fraction of the time it otherwise would have taken. The sound or the music of a place was the key to unlocking the riddle of the sanctity of the land and generating an interpretation of why the ancient peoples and the modern visitor alike hold Sedona as a sacred place.

From this quick examination of the role of the qualities of form, color and sound we can now return to the chakras and perhaps find a way toward an understanding of them.

The Base Chakra

Each chakra works at a different vibrational level and is attuned to a different color, sound or other quality at specific points in the spectrum of frequencies of creation. The base chakra, for example, vibrates at the longest frequency level and is associated with the well-being or the basic survival of the physical body. Its color vibration is red, and it is the root, the source of energy that we can draw from the earth.

In the Sedona Landscape Temple the location of the frequencies of the base chakra are roughly in the triangle of Courthouse Rock, Lee Mountain and the Twin Buttes, and are focussed on the peaks in the center of this area. As

was suggested in the chapter on the pentagram, this is an area concerned with the source of power, with emergence and with the law of the working of the human and the natural worlds. These are essential for our co-existence and survival on earth. This would be a place to visit if you are dealing with these issues. No one lives in the area.

By following the trail that runs from just below the Chapel of the Holy Cross to the Twin Buttes it is possible to pass through the break in the rock formations there and go deep into the canyons beyond. This is a secluded place of powerful beauty. The numerous spires and towers of red rock and above them, sheer cliffs of golden stone are all very evocative of the nature of the base chakra. More on this area in the second part of the chapter.

The Sacral or Sex Chakra

This chakra is located on the Twin Buttes in the center of the landscape pentagram. It includes the Madonna Rock and her partner. The vibrational frequencies of the sacral chakra are quickened from those of the base chakra and are concerned with the physical body as well as with courage, confidence, creativity and self-motivation. The rocks are essentially sexual in their nature through virtue of their shape, color and pairing.

The center of the landscape pentagram is the place of emergence. It is linked with procreation through the ratio of phi, the placement of the genitals in the pentagonic figure, and as a place sacred to Komwidapokuwia, the founder goddess of the Yavapai. It is this last association that accounts for the naming through place memory of the Madonna Rock, although the enthroned figures in all four of the monolithic red rock buttes are evidently feminine and this alone may account for the name. The throne is an archetypal symbol of the feminine.

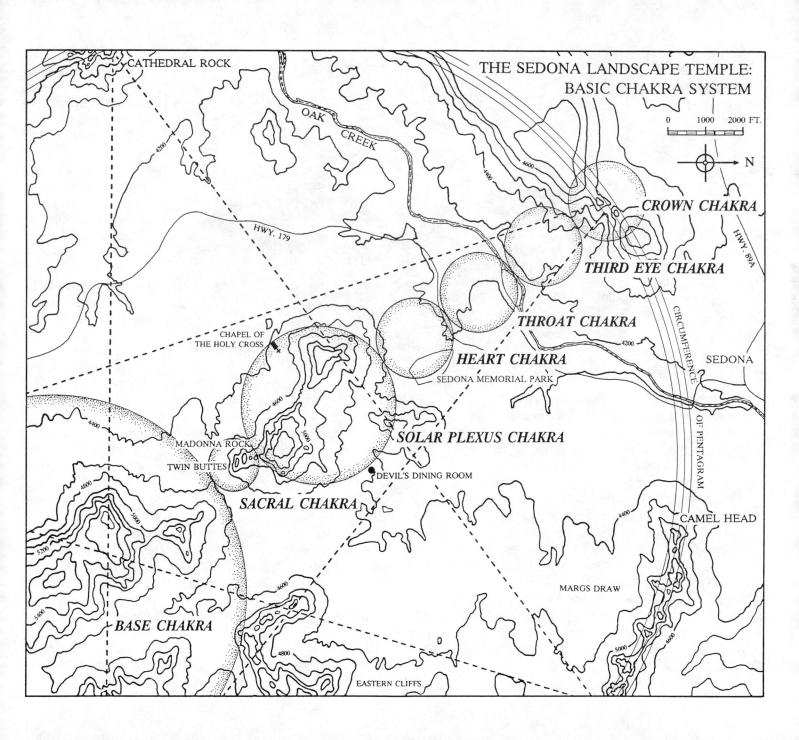

THE SEDONA LANDSCAPE TEMPLE:
BASIC CHAKRA SYSTEM

0   1000   2000 FT.

N

CATHEDRAL ROCK

OAK CREEK

HWY. 179

CHAPEL OF
THE HOLY CROSS

CROWN CHAKRA

THIRD EYE CHAKRA

HWY. 89A

THROAT CHAKRA

HEART CHAKRA

SEDONA MEMORIAL PARK

CIRCUMFERENCE OF PENTAGRAM

SEDONA

SOLAR PLEXUS CHAKRA

MADONNA ROCK
TWIN BUTTES

DEVIL'S DINING ROOM

SACRAL CHAKRA

CAMEL HEAD

MARGS DRAW

BASE CHAKRA

EASTERN CLIFFS

This would be a place to visit in order to reconnect with one's sensual nature and motivating energy. Though the area it covers is smaller than that of the base and other chakras, that does not make it any less significant. The monumental nature of the buttes and the central position in the pentagram generate its power.

The Saddle beside Twin Buttes as seen from Sedona.

Solar Plexus

The chakra located in the solar plexus finds its place in this landscape system just to the northwest of the Madonna Rock. It includes the Chapel of the Holy Cross, the saddle of the two peaks which are sometimes called the Twin Buttes and the Devil's Dining Room sinkhole.

The vibrational frequencies of the solar plexus are concerned with the feeling-emotional body. They are also concerned with mental activity, but not in this aspect of the landscape chakra system we are examining. It is only in the awakened or Realized System that the full mental powers of the solar plexus become active. The four features mentioned above fall in the shape of a rough cross. The cross is a solar symbol. It is interesting that the Chapel of the Holy Cross, built by architects who studied under Frank Lloyd Wright, has taken on this name. This is another example of geomantic resonance.

With the Chapel of the Holy Cross located on one side of the chakra line and the Devil's Dining Room on the other, there is something rather fitting being expressed about the seesawing of emotion that is the experience of the unbalanced solar plexus. A visit to both these places is recommended if balance is being sought in the emotional body. But it might be helpful to think carefully about which side of the chakra line you are going to place yourself on!

The Devil's Dining Room can be found by turning at the Broken Arrow sign up Morgan Road about half a mile south of Sedona on Hwy 179. At the end of the road, follow the trail for half a mile south. If you wish to climb up into the saddle at the center of the chakra, go west from the sinkhole along the smooth, red rock outcrops and then up the wash. But be warned, the underbrush is very thick and the last part of the climb is an unmarked, slippery and steep slope. The view of Cathedral, Bell and Courthouse Rocks to the south and the rest of the Red Rock Country to the north is superb.

The Heart Chakra

The heart chakra of the landscape temple is located in the area just south of Hwy 179 and to the north of the Twin

Buttes. This is a beautiful area but quite hard to access. It is best found by entering the Sedona Memorial Park before Poco Diablo, which was an old Indian burial ground, and then walking through the rugged forest land on the right side of the Memorial Park.

On the way to visit the area one morning, I was told that a friend lay ill with a severe heart disorder. This partly left my mind, but upon walking to the center of the chakra area thoughts of him returned. Once at the center I allowed these thoughts to follow their course, and, after praying for the light of the sun to enter my heart, I stood sending my prayers for him along the axis of the chakra system in the direction of the Airport Mesa.

It felt extraordinary to stand there knowing that to my right lay an area where the dead lay buried, while to my left the life force of the sun beat down and the abundance of nature proliferated. Balanced between life and death, focussed on what was a life and death issue, I sent my friend prayers for healing.

Later that day I was taken to the house where my friend lay ill to collect medicine from his wife for a woman who was soon expecting a baby. Not only was the exchange perfectly appropriate, but to my surprise, completely unbeknownst to me, their house lay on the chakra axis not a mile from the center of the heart chakra; that is, it lay in the place to which I had directed my prayers. Such synchronicity helped me understand the geomantic potentials of the landscape temple. And there was more.

That morning, after leaving the center of the heart chakra, I had walked back to the cemetery and the first thing I saw was a bed of white quartz in the center of which someone had arranged a red rock heart. All around was evidence of loving intention.

At a grave where a man lay buried there was a space beside him for his wife. The tombstone had her name and date of birth but an, as yet, blank space for her date of death. This must have required coping with potentially overwhelming emotions. Once again I felt the power of synchronicity, for earlier that morning, before I had even known I was going to visit the Memorial Park I had worked through strong feelings of life, death and fear of loss.

These issues of life passage, of birth and of death, are the ones to be worked within this area. I personally realized that between the oscillation of the feelings - the systole and the diastole of the human heart - was a place where the eternity of oneness that the tombstones expressed did not necessarily consist of a physical togetherness, but lay in the freedom which was in letting go, in the compassionate love that honored the free spirit of all beings.

The Throat Chakra

Just to the north of Poco Diablo resort, between Hwy 179 and Oak Creek lies the area designated as the throat chakra in this landscape system. It is an area that is being encroached upon by roads and development. This itself is not without significance, for it shows the need for and the importance of communication to our age.

The center of the chakra can be reached by walking from the top of Bowstring Road which runs up beside the Chapel of the Red Rocks. This is a residential area and visitors should therefore be discreet. It is only a short walk and a small climb but the view all around is good.

From the flat top of the hill at the center of the chakra, the presence of Hwy 179 is made known by the noise of the traffic. The road runs almost completely around one half of the hill. As one descends in the other direction this noise disappears, until after a small dropoff, the sound of Oak Creek can be heard coming through the trees. Oak Creek cradles one half of the area that forms the throat chakra as Hwy 179 cradles the other half.

The contrast between the sounds of the road and the river is dramatic. Oak Creek gurgles, happily splashes and in places thun-

Oak Creek.

As I stood in a natural circle of stones at the center of the throat chakra, I sensed the importance of speaking and of listening, of keeping still and still moving. The sound of "O" came to represent the full circle and the free passage through which both modalities could move.

The throat chakra provides the link between the mental

ders over the red rocks. The highway grinds, rattles and roars as the traffic passes along it. The two places are the antithesis of each other. One is melodious while the other is cacophonous. One communicates by allowing a means of passage from one place to another and by carrying a sound with it, while the other communicates through a combination of sounds, which although created by a flowing medium, remain constant in one place.

On the day I visited the throat chakra, I realized that the issues dealt with here involved sending messages and receiving them, not only talking but listening, remaining still in order to hear. It was possible to sit still and hear the river's song created by the dynamic movement of the water or to move with one's own message; which, if the metaphor of the car is taken further, may mean drowning out the sounds of others while being encased in a solid medium which does not allow other sounds to enter in.

and the physical-emotional bodies. Through balance here the energies of the whole body connect. In working with this chakra, a common tendency is to babble, not listen. The result is that instead of thinking with our mental and feeling faculties combined we think only with the faculties of the speaking function. That is, in terms of opposites; yes and no, right and wrong, good and evil, the dualities which form the structure of language. It is by O-pening the throat that the full nature of being can be appreciated, the full circle be drawn, which may mean holding together two apparently irreconcilable concepts and learning to live with paradox.

To reach this section of Oak Creek, which is one of the most beautiful in the area, take Brewer Road to the end and walk down the path which leads to the river. The south bank is an island, for a small stream breaks off here and rejoins the creek further downstream. It is difficult to gain access from the southeast bank.

The Third Eye

Between Oak Creek and the Airport Mesa just beyond the development known as the Palisades lies the third eye chakra of this landscape system. It is not easily accessible. A way might be found down from the airport, but it is better to take the Forest Service Road which runs just above Oak Creek at the end of Brewer Road and then cut directly up the hillside. Originally and not so long ago, access was possible by walking the wash which runs up to the twin hills of the Airport Mesa, but the Palisades development has now blocked this route.

The third eye is important as the connecting link between the physical, emotional and mental bodies and the crown chakra. It is sometimes shown as a spiral, or a fiery horn emerging from the forehead. It finds its expression in the unicorn, a magical creature which inspires dreams and visions. The unicorn calls forth the greatest purity and the highest aspirations.

The third eye also deals with issues of perception, intuition, focus and synthesis. For these reasons this chakra is usually located at the high altar of cathedrals based upon the structure of the chakra system. Not on the altar itself but just in front of it, the place where the priest would stand when lifting up and consecrating the sacraments of bread and wine. This is where the elements of earth are prepared to meet the elements of spirit and the magical process of transubstantiation can take place.

When I visited the area of the third eye chakra, there, lying on the ground, was a long spiral shell reminiscent of the horn of the unicorn, although I do not know from which creature it came. Whatever the unicorn is, it felt present that day as my intention was focussed on completing the journey along the chakra system and visiting the crown.

The Crown Chakra

The crown chakra of this section of the landscape temple is located upon the twin hills in the saddle of the Airport Mesa. The area can be reached quite easily from the Airport Road, which lies half a mile west from the junction of Hwy 89A and Hwy 179. It is quite a climb if one wishes to reach the summits of the mesa on either side, but the views make the effort worthwhile.

It is said in the Hopi legends that Palatkwapi - the Red City of the South - was a place of great teaching on many levels. At the highest level, initiates were taught about the "open door" on top of their heads and "how to keep it open and so converse with their Creator." (Chief Tawakwaptiwa in the *Book of the Hopi*.) The twin hills of the Airport Mesa form the landscape correspondence to the "open door" of the crown chakra.

The fine qualities of the Crown Chakra have been recognized in the traditions of many cultures. It has been seen as the place of egress of the soul after death, as the place of the entry of spirit - often in the form of a bird - and as the seat of wisdom and compassion. Customs associated with these qualities of the crown chakra range from the wearing of crowns of precious stones or of feathered headdresses, to artists' renditions of haloes, to the wearing of hair in a certain way. Once the "open door" to the crown chakra has been realized, it is often depicted as a thousand petaled lotus or as some other multifaceted form.

In the greater picture of all the elements of the Sedona Landscape Temple, the twin hills of the Airport Mesa are the place where the pentagram meets the hexagram and the path of the Great Bird intersects their common axis and the line of the chakras at right angles. It is a place of great power and significance.

Naturally, when I visited the airport as a culmination of a period spent investigating the other six chakras, I had my expectations. I was not disappointed. But, as is usual with all these things, the signs from spirit did not come the way I thought they would.

Arriving early in the morning to avoid the heat of a long, dry summer day I parked below the hill and made my way

The opening in the Twin Hills of the Airport Mesa. The Crown Chakra of the Basic System. Thunder Mountain lies beyond.

up the dusty trail. The birds were very busy. On the crest of the mesa, jet black ravens lifted off the bare branches of an ancient juniper to circle around to a vantage point on the other side. They watched closely. Their cry was mocking. The trickster was afoot.

After a while signs of synchronicity began to emerge. A golden orange golf ball in the center of the chakra parodied the thousand petals of the lotus with its tiny facets. Then a long discarded corn cob came to light. Plainly, the finding of the "open door" was not scheduled to be an event of great seriousness and ceremony.

The ravens laughed and, close by, hummingbirds fought fiercely over territory as the orange golf ball was placed in the center of a spiral labyrinthine path drawn in the dust. The golf ball was then covered with earth, symbolizing a

means of leaving unsustainable technology behind. Then the corn cob was placed at the exit of the maze. The act, in its very simplicity, carried a promise of emergence into new life.

There was nothing great to do, no complex rituals to perform. Coyotes yipped and howled in the canyon below as an airplane passed low in the sky overhead. Golf balls and corn cobs and coyotes were enough of a reminder that the pathways between the world of spirit and the world of matter were already wide open.

A song was sung as a gift to the place honoring all the animals. At the verse dedicated to the bird people, a huge turkey vulture came flying down the dragon line from the northwest. It skimmed between the trees just above the red earth and passed by on its undeviating course not a dozen feet away. Every detail of its feathers and ugly red head could be seen. A moment later its mate appeared and the two circled upwards in the air currents of the canyon. In several native traditions the turkey vulture is considered equal in medicine power to the eagle. There was no doubt that its flight along the axis of the chakra system was a powerful sign from spirit that the doorway between the worlds stands open.

CHAKRA CHART

CHAKRA	COLOUR	TONE	LOCATION IN BODY	DOMAIN	PROPERTY	SANSKRIT NAME	TREE OF LIFE	LOC. IN BASIC SYSTEM	LOC. IN RLZD. SYSTEM
CROWN	PURPLE VIOLET	'I'	ABOVE THE HEAD	SPIRITUAL	ENLIGHTENMENT WISDOM	SAHASRARA	AIN SOPH	AIRPORT MESA	LONG CANYON
			— PINEAL —				— KETHER —		
THIRD EYE	INDIGO	'E'	PITUITARY	MENTAL	INTUITION VISUALISATION FOCUS	AJNA	BINAH-CHOKMA	BETWEEN AIRPORT & OAK CREEK	GRASSY KNOLLS
THROAT	BLUE	'O'	THYROID	MENTAL	COMMUNICATION KNOWLEDGE	VISUDDHA	DAATH	OAK CREEK	THUNDER MTN./ DEVIL'S BRIDGE
HEART	GREEN	'A'	HEART THYMUS	EMOTIONAL	LOVE COMPASSION	ANAHATA	GEBORAH-CHESED	MEMORIAL GROUNDS	SUGARLOAF (HORUS ROCK)
							— TIPHARETH —		
SOLAR PLEXUS	YELLOW	'OO'	ADRENALS PANCREAS	EMOTIONAL	EMOTIONS INTELLECT	MANIPURA	HOD-NETZACH	THE SADDLE (HOLY CROSS CHAPEL-DEVIL'S DINING ROOM)	AIRPORT MESA
									— OAK CREEK —
SACRAL OR SEX	ORANGE	'U'	GONADS SPLEEN	PHYSICAL	ENERGY MOTIVATION	SVADISTHANA	YESOD	TWIN BUTTES	THE SADDLE
									— TWIN BUTTES —
BASE OR ROOT	RED	'M'	PERINEUM	PHYSICAL	SURVIVAL POWER GROUND	MULADHARA	MALKUTH	SOUTHEAST OF TWIN BUTTES	SOUTHEAST OF TWIN BUTTES

Part II - The Realized Chakra System

When we deny there is consciousness in nature,
we also deny consciousness to the worlds we find
by going THROUGH nature; and we end with only one world,
the world of McDonald's, and that one is exploitable.

Robert Bly. "News of the Universe" 1980.

Introduction

Tribal societies throughout the world have always held certain places in the land to be sacred. These are places used for purposes such as ceremony, initiation, vision quest, the making of vows, prayer and story telling. The features of the sacred environment are invariably distinctive and have their origins in a mythology of creation involving ancestral, ethereal or totemistic beings.

Visiting the sacred site reestablishes communication with the time of origin, with the spirit world - the "Dreamtime" of the Australian Aborigine. Through the recognition of such places set aside from "normal" time and space, the landscape is ordered into a total symbolic cosmology in which people can understand the nature of the cosmos and where they are and who they are within it. Without the acknowledgement of such places, the cosmos becomes chaotic, lacking in sanctity and often totally profaned. Although it is an admirable ideal, it is hard to carry the concept of "everywhere is sacred" into the details of everyday life.

The sacred place, set apart from everyday life, perhaps marked by petroglyphs, rock paintings or simply by the numinous qualities of the place, and protected by the mythological stories of the people, is found among all of the traditional cultures of the Southwest. The Yavapai and the Red Rock Country are no exception to this.

In the myths and legends of Komwidapokuwia and Skatakaamcha we find a classic example of the origin, nature and power of a sacred place. The story of Komwidapokuwia's emergence from the first world and the creation of the people of the second world and that of Skatakaamcha's search for his father, the placing of Sun medicine in one side of his body and Cloud medicine in the other side, his descent to the land and the impressing of his body upon it, are classic expressions of the origin of the symbolic and potent nature of the sacred landscape.

Through going to the appropriate place and singing the appropriate songs, the communication established with the spirit world assures integration back into the whole, back into balance and also the giving of the "medicine power" needed for healing, rain and so on. The body of Skatakaamcha impressed upon the land assures that this is so.

The first part of this chapter suggested one such figure impressed into the earth. This was the Basic Chakra System composed of the figure in the pentagram. The indications are however, that there are other figures or chakra systems in the Sedona landscape.

In the Yavapai legends the passage from sky to earth, from matter to spirit and vice versa, is of vital concern. And following the idea that Sedona, like Palatkwapi, is a place to learn about the "open door" at the top of the head, a second chakra system integrating the pentagram and the hexagram is now presented.

In alchemical literature on music and its relation to the terrestrial and the heavenly spheres it was said that the whole could be likened to a monochord (a fretted, single stringed instrument) of two octaves. The first octave corresponded to the terrestrial and the second to the heavenly sphere. However, when the second octave was played it was not simply a progression up the scale, rather it was as though an impediment, such as a finger that had been resting on the middle of the string, was lifted and the whole string played. Thus, both octaves shared a common base point.

In the same way as the monochord, the second or the Realized Chakra System has its root chakra located in the same area as in the Basic System. But the crown chakra instead of being on the Airport Mesa now lies further along the dragon line in the Long Canyon area and the Airport Mesa becomes the new solar plexus chakra. (See the map for the location of the other chakras.)

The reader may prefer not to follow this design. There are several variations on chakra systems available and a different system may be applied. For example, the student of the Kabbalah may have noticed a similarity between the juxtaposition of the pentagram and the hexagram with the structure of the Tree of Life. The points of the geometrical figures form a good approximation of the positions of the Sephiroth. And although there may not be an exact correspondence, the passage of the Lightning Flash through the Tree of Life is often taken to illustrate the serpentine currents of energy that pass through the body and its chakra system. In this case, the places in the landscape associated with each chakra would spread over a wider area than given in the Realized System.

It would also be instructive to look at traditional Native American ways of visiting a sacred site. A visit, for example, may be preceded by fasting, sweat lodges and purification or by such activities over a certain period of time at the site. In general, "medicine," here defined as spiritual power, was honored, respected and sought after for specific ends. A shaman might visit a particular place and conduct a ceremony in order to gain medicine which then could be called upon for use in the future.

As Gifford's informants have described there were many kinds of medicine. These were available to anyone who undertook the necessary steps. Everyone could acquire shamanistic power to some degree. It is doubtful that one Yavapai shaman could acquire all the medicine power that Skatakaamcha made available. There were rain-making shamans, rattlesnake-bite shamans and so on. The medicine often required lengthy songs or prayers which had to be exact and took considerable training to learn.

It is interesting to note that usually Native American prayers are for specific goals, such as the healing of an individual, the ability to know the location of game or the well-being of someone undertaking a journey or a test. The prayers of white people are more general, for example, for the ending of world hunger and war. Could it be that the medicine power promised to lie in the earth by Skatakaamcha and "caught" by a song, is actual and quantitative rather than qualitative? One person therefore, could not handle medicine except on the specific, individual level, for the power required for, say world peace, would be beyond the limits of any one person. (However, this merely shows the importance of cooperation for the purpose of achieving goals on a global scale.)

This diagram illustrates the correspondence between the joint configuration of the hexagram and the pentagram of the Sedona Landscape Temple and the structure of the Kabbalistic Tree of Life. The bold line shows the Lightning Flash.

Planetary and chakra associations with the Sephiroth are also shown and meditation upon these throws light upon the nature of their places in the landscape. Tiphareth, for example, as the Sun, corresponds to the solar plexus of the Realized System and the crown chakra of the Basic System. Chesed, as Jupiter, relates closely to the energies of Thunderbird Rock.

Dion Fortune, the great writer on the occult, had this to say regarding the Tree of Life:

"...the Tree consists of the two Pillars of Polarity and the Path of Equilibrium between them. The true secret of natural goodness lies in the recognition of the contending rights of the Pairs of Opposites; there is no such antinomy as between Good and Evil, but only the balance between two extremes."

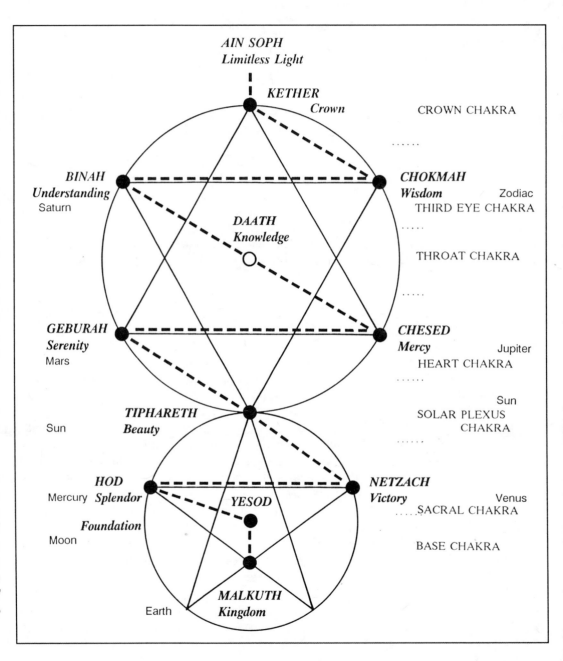

AIN SOPH
Limitless Light

KETHER
Crown   CROWN CHAKRA

BINAH
Understanding   CHOKMAH
Saturn   Wisdom   Zodiac
                                 THIRD EYE CHAKRA

DAATH
Knowledge   THROAT CHAKRA

GEBURAH   CHESED
Serenity   Mercy   Jupiter
Mars   HEART CHAKRA

                                                 Sun
                                 SOLAR PLEXUS
TIPHARETH   CHAKRA
Sun   Beauty

HOD   NETZACH
Mercury Splendor   Victory   Venus
                  YESOD   SACRAL CHAKRA
Foundation
Moon   BASE CHAKRA

                  MALKUTH
Earth   Kingdom

The story of Skatakaamcha impressing himself "belly down" upon the earth with the various medicines present in either side of his body would lead us to see the land to the right of the central line of the chakras as belonging to the Sun and that to the left as belonging to the Cloud. That is, if this interpretation of where he lies is correct. With this in mind, and with his advice "sing my songs," a journey was made along the line of the Realized Chakra System as had been done for the Basic Chakra System.

Sound became an essential part of attuning to a site; most often the voice, but occasionally a flute, ocarina or some light percussion such as a rattle was used. If it felt appropriate a song would be sung after a short ceremony honoring the place, the elements and the directions.

There now follows a necessarily subjective description of the seven vital centers of the Realized Chakra System in the hope that it provides a way for visitors to relate to the specific locales for themselves. This is by no means definitive, nor a "how to do it," and therefore may be skimmed over by those seeking factual knowledge or who do not wish to form preconceptions prior to their visit to the place.

The Root and Sacral Chakras - Twin Buttes

Follow the trail marked by cairns that runs southeast from just below the Chapel of the Holy Cross. After about half a mile the trail turns east through a narrow valley beside the Twin Buttes. Allow a good half hour to make this part of the journey for the trail winds about and the views are distracting.

After the magnificent pair of buttes that mark the point of connection between the root and the sacral chakras it is possible to go through a gate and pick up the trail which leads into the secluded valley below Lee Mountain. This, or the jeep trail from Broken Arrow to Submarine Rock, is the only approach to the rock formations that form the heart of the root chakra, for sheer cliffs guard its southern and western flanks.

This little walked, but fairly easy trail passes through a delightful forest of dwarf Arizona cypress, manzanita and agave but finally peters out to all but the most determined bushwhackers. It may be possible to cross the ridges and emerge North of Courthouse Rock or even to try for the summit of Lee Mountain but I've never attempted it.

On the day I visited, I walked for maybe a mile past the Twin Buttes. The sun was setting and the shadows lay long across the valley floor. It was cool, late in the year, and my overwhelming impression was that of energy, of vital life force. The image of a lion came to mind. This was echoed by the massive formation of golden Coconino sandstone which dominates the southern skyline from the area of the Chapel of the Holy Cross and which resembles the form of a crouching lion. This formation is approximately at the center of the root chakra.

The red and gold glow from the cliffs in the valley reminded me of the Yavapai calling themselves the People of the Sun. But here, rather than from the sky, the fire felt to be coming from within, from the source that was sustaining my life and the lives of those around me.

This life energy felt inexhaustible and capable of achieving things that were not ordinarily possible. For example, healing a wound in a very short time. Blood flowed from a cut on the hand of my companion, echoing the red cliffs in the sunset. And in the wound itself, in the reflections that it brought, there was also power. Not only the power to heal, but the power of the creation of life, as signified for instance by menstrual blood.

Twin Buttes from the east.

At length, the sun set to the southwest over Cathedral Rock and the shadows of the Twin Buttes rose up like two horns on the sheer canyon wall below Lee Mountain. The cliffs glowed with an inner fire and the twin shadows were perfect in their symmetry. It was like watching the epiphany of some forgotten god.

The sensations evoked were ones of duality and of balance. These may be the issues to work with here. To be made useful, the fire of raw sexual energy has to be taken beyond the realm of attraction and repulsion into the state of balance. I was reminded of the message of the man and the woman standing back to back in the central spires of Cathedral Rock.

It felt appropriate to sing a chant my companion had put together in the Yavapai tongue which honored the fire of the sun. The words are

Ya-pe-i Hi-wa-ya In-ya

which mean, the spirit heart of the sun. The basic undertone was a low "mmm...."

It seems significant that the basic raw energy encountered at the root chakra is so intimately connected with the energy of the sacral chakra that it is hard to distinguish between them. The approaches to the root chakra are along trails that have first passed through the sacral chakra. And at the towering monoliths which mark where the chakras touch, this connection is most apparent. From the east the two spires beside the Twin Buttes take on the appearance of lovers in close embrace. One of these spires is the Madonna Rock.

Here, beside the Twin Buttes, the differences between male and female seemed to be highly accentuated. Unless worked out, these differences would predominate in games of love and war. And yet through the balance of those powerful forces, the cup that is constantly being spilled in criticism and argument could be set upright and the horns of balance and inner power worn with pride once more.

At the entrance of the valley just to the west of the Twin Buttes there is a stack of red rock on the other side of the wash which closely resembles a sphinx. It looks toward the sunset and is complete with outstretched paws and Egyptian headdress. The lion energy returned strongly. My companion remarked that the lion is to the sphinx as the potential human is to the evolved or realized human. In ancient Egypt the sphinx symbolized truth. It pointed out where we hold shadows inside ourselves. If there is projection, anger or fear then these will be intensely magnified in the sex chakra and there will be imbalance. The sphinx has aligned the raw, instinctive energy of the lion and in balance and fearlessness has taken it on to the next stage.

The sun set quickly and it was quite dark on the winding trail back to the road.

The Solar Plexus - The Airport Mesa

The Airport Mesa is one of Sedona's most visited and easily accessible power spots. At the top of the hill, about half a mile west of the junction of Hwy 89A and Hwy 179 turn south onto Airport Road. Just past the cattle grid are several parking places from which it is a short climb to the rock outcrops that lie at the center of the Airport Mesa.

The Mesa is a good sunrise and sunset viewing place. The summer solstice sun rises over Schnebly Hill to the northeast and sets over Boynton Canyon and Bear Mountain to the northwest. The equinoxes and the cross-quarter days are also good times to visit and observe the sun's rising and setting points on the horizon. The cross-quarter days are the calendar points midway between solstice and equinox. These are the old Celtic fire festivals of Samhain (Halloween), Imbolc (Candlemas), Beltaine (May Day) and Lughnasad (Lammas). Many European sacred sites are oriented to these four declinations.

To the southeast there is a view over Oak Creek of the huge symmetrical masses of rock sometimes known as the Twin Buttes. This is to the confusion of the visitor and resident of Sedona alike; for that name belongs to the red rock buttes which lie below the formations and are invisible from the airport. Perhaps the name is interchangeable. Cradled in the saddle of the two rock formations can be seen the peaks that lie in the area defined in this system as the root chakra.

It was a winter day when I visited the Airport Mesa and at sunrise the sky above the saddle glowed with the fire of the root and sacral chakras. It felt as though the energy of those chakras was focused by the balanced symmetry of the two buttes. And as the sun rose, a line of light streamed toward the Airport Mesa, symbolizing that in the Realized Chakra System the cup of sexuality containing the vital life force has been set upright and its energy made available to the solar plexus.

This chakra then becomes the seat of emotional power. Not emotions tugging this way and that, but responding like the horse to the slightest touch of a good rider. At this stage, feelings become as thoughts, so quickly can they be articulated and directed into creative action. E-motion, conscious energy in motion. I was reminded of one of the sayings of Gurdjieff who taught that "we must learn to think where we now feel and feel where we now think."

Turning around and looking to the northeast, the bulk of Old Grayback rose into the sky. At its foot, modest in comparison, lay Sugarloaf which, according to the geometry of the chakra system, forms the center of the heart chakra. It seemed appropriate to go there immediately.

The Heart Chakra - Sugarloaf

On this occasion I drove up Mountain Shadows Road, parked at the top and followed the footpath around the eastern flank of the hill before doubling back to the summit. I knew from a previous visit that an easier trail runs from the top of Coffee Pot Drive and then up the main trail to the summit. I write "main trail to the summit," for while the north slope of the hill is the obvious ascent route - the south being precipitous - and there must have always been a path there, in recent years a bulldozer has for some obscure reason torn up the ground from top to bottom.

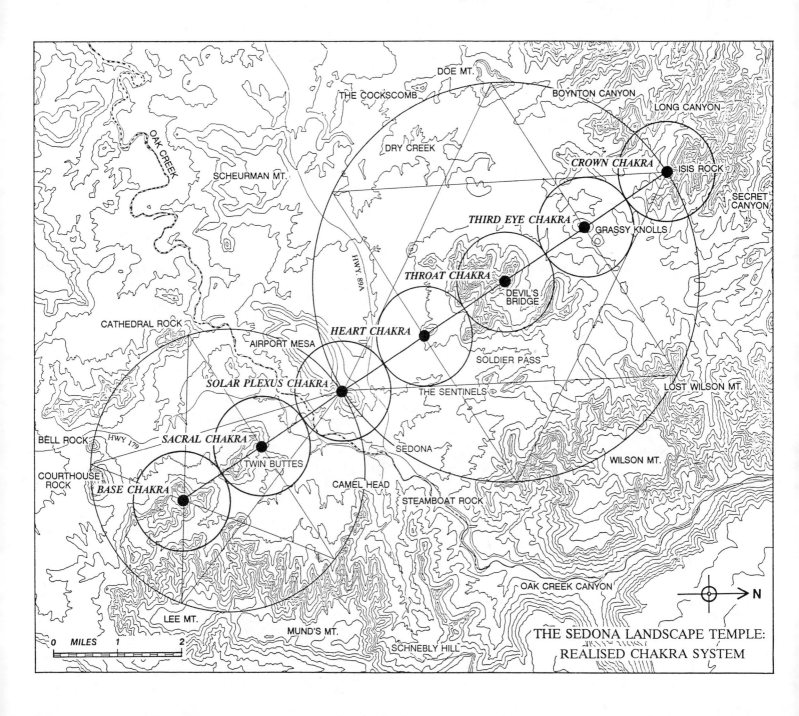

THE SEDONA LANDSCAPE TEMPLE:
REALISED CHAKRA SYSTEM

A terrible scar has been left on the hill, a scar as cruel as it is pointless, and such carelessness has already prompted littering such as does not take place at far more visited places like the airport. Campsites with broken bottles and discarded papers and utensils created the feeling that everyone wants the experience of the "feast of the heart" but this desire often manifests externally in unconscious and harmful actions. The story of the search for truth came to mind, in which, after long discussions of where to hide truth in the universe, the Powers That Be decided out of compassion to place it within the human heart.

In geomancy, the heart of the dragon - in this case the dragon being the lung mei, or ley line that forms the backbone of the chakra system - always lies on a small knoll in the center of a plain surrounded by mountains. Here, the two currents of yin, the White Tiger, and yang, the Blue Dragon, meet in terrestrial harmony.

Sugarloaf hill seems to fit these qualifications in every respect. Tree-covered, undulating land all around forms the breath of the White Tiger, while the Blue Dragon breathes powerfully from the buttes that lie in the distance.

I noticed a good east-west, therefore equinox, alignment from Chimney Rock behind which lay the Cockscomb, through Sugarloaf to Giant's Thumb and Schnebly Hill. This was confirmed by compass. The equinoxes are the times of balance between the yin and yang forces. On or around March 21 and September 21 from Sugarloaf the sun will rise over Schnebly Hill and set behind Chimney Rock and the Cockscomb. I was reminded of the sun medicine entering the right side of Skatakaamcha and felt that this would be a good place to honor the equinox sunrises.

With such powerful geomantic qualifications this seldom-visited, torn up but still beautiful little hill seems greatly undervalued. Returning to the mythology of Skatakaamcha and the spreading out and impressing of his body into the land, it is fairly easy to see how this red knoll separated from its neighbors and rounded in shape possesses the physical appearance of a human heart. I felt, as many quantum physicists are now feeling, that consciousness is inseparable from, and indeed, shapes matter, so exactly has nature made the hill in the form of a heart.

Such a concept as the body of a giant spread over the land would inevitably mean that its heart would be a place of ceremonial importance. It would be a magical center deserving great respect. Good medicine could be obtained there for physical, emotional and spiritual purification and strength. More poetically it may be a place where lovers trysts are tied. The long "A" sound came in a song.

With Horus Rock towering above Sugarloaf with its bird-like head and beak, the powers of the winged messengers of spirit felt very close to earth. There was a sense of the indomitable spirit of the golden eagle, and of the hawk; but as is often the case in the Southwest, it was those black scavengers the ravens that watched over my descent.

The Throat Chakra - Devil's Bridge

Continuing the journey along the line which runs through the center of each chakra in the Realized System the next point of call was Rainbow or Devil's Bridge. This is the closest one can get to the center of the throat chakra for the exact center, the sheer pinnacle above the bridge, would require a major expedition.

The unpaved Vultee Arch Trail off Dry Creek Road is prone to deterioration from flash floods and heavy usage. It is really only passable by off-road vehicles. Still, for the walker, the Devil's Bridge is less than two miles through gor-

Rainbow Bridge.

As one would expect from a throat chakra the echo is astonishing. Sound bounces off the canyon walls even though they are a good half mile apart. It is also a place of listening, an aspect of the throat chakra that is often overlooked as was commented on in the Basic System.

The bridge itself provides a wonderful image for meditation. Sound moves through in both directions - in and out - proving the necessity for all our faculties, especially the ears and throat, to be clear, so a similar free passage can happen within us. To be ready to play on the octave of the Realized System there has to be alignment with all the steps that have gone before. Like the steps on the trail, it is impossible to reach the ones at the top until the ones on the bottom have been climbed.

So strongly do the energies of the total geomancy of Sedona converge here - it is the hexagram's center, the serpent's heart, the throat chakra (Da'ath in the Tree of Life) - that anything less than total readiness for the place could mean considerable discomfort for a motivated but unprepared visitor. The intention of the visitor is everything.

As the center of the hexagram it is the step beyond. The point where the dilemma of the dichotomy between spirit and matter becomes absolute. There is only the way back or the way on from here. The new vessel is formed for new energies or the old remains as it is. Conversely, new energies are formed for the new vessel. The old quandary, which came first the chicken or the egg?, finds its resolution in the dynamic which takes place at this level.

"In the beginning was the Word..." is the way Scripture has it, and this is true. And there was also the power that some call the undifferentiated, primordial Great Mother, and this is true. The energy of the Word or the Logos, joins with the form or the vessel to become pure being. Spirit-Matter

geous terrain. Turn off the Vultee Arch Trail at the sign and follow the improved trail to the bridge. "Improved" is a euphemism for degraded by four wheel drive vehicles which go much further than really necessary, crushing the rocks and manzanita. However, the last quarter of a mile is a fine walk and steps have been provided for the steep parts.

joined together creates a dynamic of holism which does not and cannot put one before the other.

There is the sound, there is the instrument. There is the instrument, there is the sound. Neither emphasis on Logos orientation or chthonic orientation, on Spirit or on Matter, is relevant here. This can be seen in the legends of Komwidapokuwia and Skatakaamcha.

Komwidapokuwia is the chthonic Great Mother born from the grinding around of the metate of Black Night. Skatakaamcha is the Logos born out of the Great Mother and through whose songs the powers of the Great Mother are made manifest. "Skatakaamcha gives us everything" the Yavapai say, and "He got it all from Komwidapokuwia." The Word, or the songs of Skatakaamcha, is medicine or spiritual power. But it is from and within the Grandmother that these have substance and life.

A good metaphor of this may be the woven blanket or rug. The pattern painstakingly worked out and ordered into colors and design signifying many things needs the warp and the spun wool to be anything at all. Nature has to be gone through, not risen above, for us to become whole. Here, those who would accuse the adherents of heaven centered, Logos oriented religions of being too transcendental, and those who would accuse the adherents of earth centered, Pagan religions of being too matter bound, can find the bridge between their differences and begin to live in a way that does not divide Heaven from Earth.

The Third Eye Chakra - Grassy Knolls

Take the Dry Creek Road from Hwy 89A toward Thunder Mountain. After about three miles, just beyond the usually dry crossing of Dry Creek, turn right toward Long Canyon. The left turn goes to Boynton Canyon and to Boynton Pass and eventually to the Indian ruins at Honanki and Palatki. Not far up the Long Canyon road the two Grassy Knolls appear ahead and to the right. It's possible to park on the left hand side of the road near where the trailhead to Long Canyon is located.

The Grassy Knolls have derived their name from their smooth, rounded appearance. They lack any distinguishing feature, which makes them quite innocuous in this area where every rise has its caves, cliffs and crags of rock. They are however, harder to climb than they look. Not much grass but plenty of thorny vegetation grows on their flanks. The stone is unusually well-polished and loose. By the time I reached the top of the southerly knoll, even with perfect winter hiking weather, I felt deserving of the view of the surrounding mountains.

Looking southeast along the central axis of the chakra system it was just possible to make out the Devil's Bridge lying in the shade at the foot of the peaks of Thunder Mountain. To the northwest, Isis Rock watched from the sunlit side of Long Canyon. Being perfectly situated between these landmarks on the dragon line, I wondered what surprises would be hosted by the seemingly innocent Grassy Knolls.

On the summit of the knoll was a beautiful collection of junipers. In places they formed groves; but the fact that several of them had been hit by lightning and burnt to the ground was conducive to understanding why, for the most part, junipers prefer to stand alone. One tree had been hit so squarely by lightning that its branches had splayed out equally in all directions while its trunk had been entirely burnt away leaving nothing but a crater in the center.

Close by this tree, at the northerly end of the knoll, are two medicine wheels. They have been built side by side in such a way that their common axis lies across the dragon line. Now, in some places the proliferation of medicine wheels in the Sedona area has almost reached epidemic proportions and has detracted from the natural beauty of the place. While there is certainly a case to be made for spontaneity, it should be remembered that medicine circles were originally built by those who possessed knowledge of the subtle currents of the land, of proportion, of measure and astronomy and the ability to maintain the ceremonial purpose which kept the site alive. If these qualities are lacking it may be preferable to keep the original nature of the land intact. Well, here on the Grassy Knolls, such doubts did not arise, for this pair of circles so carefully laid out upon the ground were a most welcome addition to the natural spirit of the place.

Without saying a word, my companion took the southernmost circle and I the other. We quickly moved around them burning cedar and sage at each of the stations of the inner and outer wheels. At the same time we put back into place any of the carefully selected white quartz stones that had become dislodged. A hunter with a grim sense of humor had left a cartridge in the center of one circle and there was a coin in the other. We removed them. We did not think to ourselves or explain to each other what we were doing. We just did it. We then exchanged circles.

There came a point when we knew the work was finished. The whole thing was over very quickly and did not allow thoughts about the greater context of the temple system through which we were moving. Only upon walking back down the hill did thoughts arise.

I became aware of feeling very balanced. As though the fine tuning into a wavelength only previously roughly located had now been done. The two medicine wheels astride the chakra line had allowed subtler mechanisms beyond the conscious level to come into play. The fact we were man and woman had assisted in this tuning but I could not say exactly how. It felt connected with the promise of Skata-kaamcha, "sing around my body... and you will keep alive." And given that I had taken the sun side medicine wheel and my companion the cloud side medicine wheel, perhaps the two channels that rise up beside the central channel of the human chakra system had become balanced.

In Eastern teaching on the awakening of the power of the Kundalini that lies at the base of the spine, the two channels - the Ida and Pingala, the sun and moon lines - have to be perfectly balanced or the energy of the Kundalini will not rise exactly up the central channel of the system - the Shushumna. In Western traditions, such as the Kaballistic Tree of Life, the right and left hand sides, represented by opposing pillars of the sun and the moon, must be balanced in order for the Lightning Flash to be activated. Sometimes this is shown as a caduceus, a staff around which twin serpents are entwined.

It also came to mind that two halves cannot fight against each other when they realize that together they make a whole. The ramifications of this seemed to go beyond ourselves as male and female to the reconciliation of the two hemispheres of the brain - the logical-rational and the feeling-intuitive sides of our nature - to the polarities that dominate the entire world.

Indeed, when history looks back to this time of writing it may see that the conciliation of the two socio-economic political modes of Capitalism and Communism which have dominated the 20th century world was the issue of utmost importance. Perhaps it would be wishful thinking to imagine that the work done at the medicine wheels had anything to do with this. But I did reflect that it was both sides of the line that had to be adjusted, not just one. It is to be hoped that the capitalist world can make adaptations as great as those currently being demonstrated in the communist world for capitalism has been as equally maladjusted to the community of all beings as communism with its economic prosperity being built upon an unsustainable resource base. Be that as it may, for balancing the finer centers of the being, the two Grassy Knolls in the center of the Dry Creek area function admirably. From here the dragon line moves onward, toward and into Long Canyon proper.

The Crown Chakra - Long Canyon

It is difficult to describe the full beauty and power of the mountains and canyons that lie to the northwest of Sedona. Once upon a time the whole area came up for consideration as Secret Mountain National Park. Although that idea was shelved, a considerable area was designated as wilderness, which was probably the best protection from development it could have received. As it is, Boynton Canyon provides a resort facility for enjoyment of the rugged terrain and the entrance of Long Canyon possesses several roads going nowhere and the remains of half-built dwellings from an uncompleted development.

From afar, the seams of rock piled atop one another, red to gold to orange to white, appear like a wall with a relatively level top. But as one approaches, the wall breaks up and reveals deep canyons many miles long, precipitous gorges, lushly wooded mountain slopes and separate peaks rising thousands of feet into the sky. If one were to see a vision of paradise, this would be it. The Sinagua Indians apparently felt so too, for they chose to build many dwellings in every canyon despite the limited availability of water. The cliff dwellings in Boynton Canyon are relatively accessible; but everywhere, secreted away under recesses, higher up than any casual visitor would go, are many dwellings well-built in stone. (See pictures on pages v and 53.)

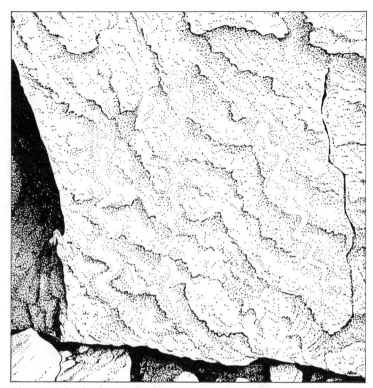

Pictographs in Long Canyon.

Secret Canyon, as the name suggests, is quite remarkable for its hidden entrances and great length from end to end. There is a trail through from Dry Creek to Loy Canyon and the Honanki cliff dwellings there. These ruins with an occupancy of between 200 and 400 people make it the largest center in the area. And Secret Canyon, with its many ruins, may once have been a busy thoroughfare.

In the center of this mass of winding, tree-filled canyons rise the peaks of Bear Mountain to the south, Maroon Mountain to the east and Secret Mountain to the north and west. Many towers and pinnacles lie in between. All are invariably capped with trees and vegetation, including ponderosa pine and stands of quite imposing Douglas fir. There tends to be a lot of Arizona cypress in the canyon bottoms along with some alligator bark juniper, pinyon pine, oak varieties and a thick understorey of manzanita, chaparral and on the more exposed rock surfaces, prickly pear, yucca and agave. All these plants would have been very useful to the early inhabitants of the canyons.

From any point in the canyon this vegetation creeping up the far-distant slopes, dappled with shades of light and dark, lends a luster to the scene that nourishes the eye and inspires feelings of well-being and happiness. Nothing is lacking in these richly adorned canyons of delight.

It takes about an hour to walk along the easy trail to the canyon itself. A brisk walker could do it in less. But why hurry? Every time I have walked just a little way into Long Canyon five hours has always flown by of its own accord by the time I've returned to the trailhead. Take lots of water, especially in summer. If any hiking off the trail is going to happen, wear adequate clothing. Being hot is definitely better than being cut and limited to where one can go. On the other hand, off-trail hiking may be a thing of the past. There are too few natural habitats remaining in the area, and heavy boots in the wrong place might wipe out the last of a plant community or disrupt a creature's breeding cycle.

A good point to aim for is Isis Rock, the topmost point in the hexagram and the Crown Chakra of the Realized System. The 200 foot tall tripartite red rock dominates the length of the trail leading into the canyon. Its gesture of hands lifted to touch the temples creates a feeling of far-seeing and inner knowing. It must stand a good 100 feet clear of the rock face, which then rises 1200 feet almost perpendicularly behind it to form a square-topped tower - though temple may be the better description - of creamy Coconino sandstone. I do not know when the name Isis Rock was originally given but it is the name currently in use and I know of none other. In the Egyptian pantheon, Isis is Queen of Heaven.

By climbing the wash which lies at the foot of Isis Rock it is possible to walk along a recess at the back of which is a layer of soft rock. This oozes enough moisture to support a community of maidenhair fern. These however, were struggling at the end of the driest year for 50 years. I had seen a similar feature at Loy Butte, Honanki, not long before. There the water was flowing at about a drip a second, definitely enough to support a small group of people.

In Boynton Canyon several of the cliff dwellings possess their own little pools filled by seepage. Knowledge of such minute sources of water would have been carefully preserved among the Sinagua and later Yavapai Indians. Of course, after rains there are many places where water can be collected and at times the washes in the canyon bottoms are transformed into thundering torrents.

Earlier, in fact just about a year to the day, I had hypothesized on the basis of the landscape hexagram, that shrines equivalent to the present day Hopi Snake Clan would be found on or near the six points of the figure. Around Thunderbird Rock there are ruins that have a ceremonial feel about them and this is also the case for ruins on Doe Mountain. It was to my delight, therefore, that I was able to find ruins around this point of the hexagram, which moreover, had pictographs of snakes on the rock walls nearby. The pictographs are painted in white and are accompanied by several crosses.

Archaeologists, like J.W. Fewkes, following the military lead, called some of the fresher pictographs "Apache," but the presence of the floriated cross makes them more likely to be Yavapai. If they are not Yavapai then they are older, perhaps contemporary with the final period of occupation by the Sinagua around 1350. At Palatki, the white pictographs have a later feel about them than the others which are often colored. But there is at least one case where a sunwheel design of possible antiquity has almost faded away, and another, similar but much later, has been painted beside it. Here, it seems, the Yavapai are renewing ancient designs.

The cross itself has ancient antecedents, as do the snakes, while a third motif, the outline of a hand is universal. At Isis Rock, as all over the Southwest, a hand was placed on the rock while pigment was sprayed from a tube or directly from the mouth over it. When the hand was withdrawn its silhouette remained on the stone.

Isis Rock on the north wall of Long Canyon.

From the red rock benches around the foot of Isis Rock the views across the canyon and out across Dry Creek to Thunder Mountain and Cathedral Rock beyond were a joy to behold. Hawks wheeled far below, catching the light on their backs as the sun's rays streamed through the vales in the south wall of the canyon. One hawk rose up suddenly from below, lifted by the updraft of the heat on the north wall and was 30 feet overhead before deciding intruders were about and veering back down and out of sight.

The pilgrimage was at an end and it felt like a beginning. Somewhere, far above, in a tiny crevice on a rock face, a drop of water fell slowly down. Then another and then another. They carved out, over the aeons, a small womb space. And, at times, when they were in flood, they carved the overhanging walls of the canyon itself. These curled softly in to embrace the seeds of life. Soil caught in the lip of the womb and the seeds grew there and tumbled down the mountainside cloaking it in green trees.

Then a creature rose up from among the trees. Then another and another, filling the earth. Then the people came up, one after another. Some brought fire into the overhanging curtains of stone and called it home. And they left the imprints of their hands on the walls of the canyon to show that they had been there and to show the hand of the Great Mystery from which they had come. And finally, the earth which bore them closed around them and took them back within.

We shall not cease from exploration
And the end of all our exploring
Will be to arrive where we started
And know the place for the first time.

We had completed our cycle, the earth lay in majestic beauty before us, around us. The sun dropped below the rim of the south wall sending rays up to greet the rising moon. We scrambled down into the shadow of the valley floor and took the Long Canyon trail home.

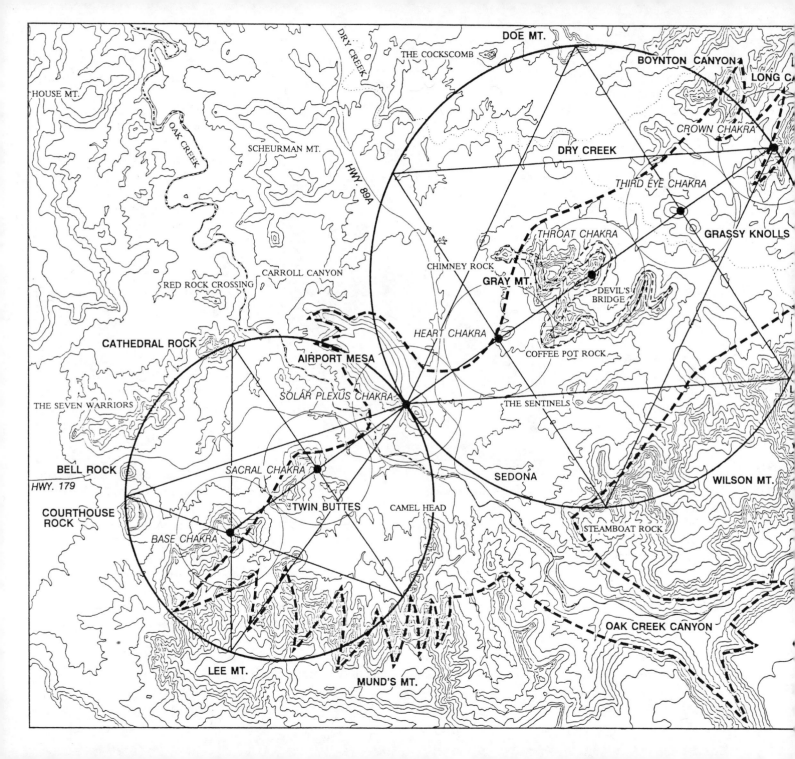

SECRET CANYON

MOGOLLON RIM

N MT.

EAST POCKET

HWY. 89A

0   MILES   1   2

E SEDONA LANDSCAPE TEMPLE:

N OF COMBINED GEOMANTIC ELEMENTS

Chapter 10

THE FLIGHT OF THE BIRD

I am circling around God, around the ancient tower,
And I have been circling for a thousand years,
And I still don't know if I'm a falcon,
Or a storm, or a great song.
Rainer Maria Rilke. "I Live My Life" 1899.
(Translation by Robert Bly.)

The Resolution of 5 and 6

The final map shows the main elements of the Sedona Landscape Temple combined together. To look more closely at the bird, the Yavapai legends speak of a dove, and strictly speaking, the beak shaped by the ridges running southwest from the Airport Mesa does not assume a hooked form. The bird also has the quality of being reversible. That is, either wing can be seen to be toward or away from the onlooker. It can be visualized from above or from below. It is not still.

The bird most easily falls into the family of accipiters: hawks and harriers, possessing the features of large wings relative to body size and spreading wingtip feathers. It also has a resemblance to an eagle but the wings may be too small and the tail feathers may not form a large enough fan, unless they are being viewed from the side. It may also be a crow or a raven but again the tail feathers do not form a fan. The whole question of identification arises again if the tail feathers are seen to extend into Mund's and Oak Creek Canyons to form a swallow tail. Then I do not know what bird resembles the figure at all. Some kites have forked tails but not spreading wing tips.

At first glance people have commented that the bird in the landscape is a dove, a phoenix, an eagle or a hawk. I prefer a hawk of a narrow tailed variety of which there are many in the area: Cooper's Hawk, Northern Goshawk, Marsh Hawk (Harrier) and Sharp-shinned Hawk. Yet searching for

Thunderbird Rock (Steamboat Rock) from the south. Beyond it is Wilson Mountain and the buttes around the sixth point of the Hexagram.

through the awareness of natural law as expressed by the pentagram and becomes fully divine through acceptance of the energy of spirit.

In the landscape figure one wing of the bird lies within the pentagram, the other wing within the hexagram. The bend of the wing on the front edge is defined in both cases by the rock formations that form the center of the geometrical figures. Where the two wings reconnect with the body near the tail feathers lie two prominent red rock formations which mark the head of Oak Creek Canyon.

To the north, Steamboat Rock can be seen as a gigantic bird emerging from the ground with wings outstretched, hence Thunderbird Rock. To the south, Giant's Thumb appears from some angles as an owl with folded wings. Both buttes determine the turning point of the wings exactly. As is clear from the map, the zigzagging lines of the promontories and canyons to the northwest and the southeast define the wingtip feathers of a bird in full flight.

a positive identification beyond that of "bird" may be unnecessary. The significance of the bird lies in its meaning, not in its categorization.

In Chapter 6 the principles associated with the five of the pentagram and the six of the hexagram were discussed. The five was seen to signify the human world and the six the world of spirit. Through the development of human consciousness the doorway to spirit may be opened. This is geomantically represented by the narrow opening between the twin hills of the Airport Mesa. Here the blending of the human and the divine selves can take place. Spirit comes into form through the gateway of the hexagram and becomes fully present in the human body. The body awakens

The Great Bird captures the geomantic essence of the Red Rock Country. In many ways it is the spirit of Oak Creek, emerging from Oak Creek Canyon, spreading its wings and continuing in water-sculpted forms toward the river's final destination. The precise patterns formed by the river have demonstrated the consciousness of nature.

It is to the Airport Mesa that our attention can now turn. In this area lies the convergence point of the giant bird and the two geometrical figures. This "hub" delineates the bird's neck and throat and the point from which the leading edges of the wings emerge. It is the point of balance created by the intersection of the bird and the line which forms the common axis of both circles and the landscape chakra systems. It is where the consciousness of nature and the consciousness of humanity meet.

As shown in Chapter 5 the animal world stands between the mineral, plant and human worlds. We find within it the exemplar model of all mediation. The animals are agents of transformation, demonstrating in their bodies and in their actions the basic patterns of the universe, in essence: movement, measure and balance.

Animals mediate not only between us and the world of nature but also between us and the world of spirit. Their patterns of movement, measured action and balance show them to be in perfect accord with the divine will for terrestrial harmony. The symmetry of the birds in their flight, the measure of the movement of their wings, the beauty of their songs and the perfect balance of their bodies reveals the birds as the ultimate mediator between us and the spirit worlds.

Like the optical illusion of the transparent cube, the reversible nature of the Great Bird, shifting in perspective from above or from below, indicates its mediating role between the spheres of the pentagram and the hexagram of the Sedona Landscape Temple. The geomancy of the bird reveals that in order to expand our consciousness to include the realm of spirit, we have first to have made the journey through nature.

The opening in Airport Mesa. The point of balance between the geometrical and animal figures in the Sedona Landscape. Cathedral Rock lies in the distance.

In ancient Egypt the embodiment of sovereignty - or the royal double - within the new pharaoh was achieved at the coronation through the descent of Ra, the Solar Deity, in the form of a hawk. The hawk was the form of Horus, the son of the great goddess Isis, and also the reincarnation of her lover Osiris. In Egyptian mythology Isis and her child, Horus, sail over the flooded land in a wooden ark, seeking the fragments of Osiris.

Isis and Osiris are the primordial ancestors. Although Isis continues through parthenogenesis - as indeed it appears in human life where women give birth to women who give birth to women - Osiris dies and is reborn continually. This is the path of the hero - the dying and the rising god.

Horus represents Osiris reborn but is not Osiris. Rather, Horus signifies the regenerative principle which makes it possible for Osiris to live again, the principle through which the pharaohs receive both the sovereignty and the power of Ra.

The Yavapai - People of the Sun - legend of the girl Komwidapokuwia and the bird set adrift in a log boat during the flood is equivalent to the story of Isis and Horus. The old world of Osiris has come to an end. Komwidapokuwia - Isis - and the bird - Horus - are carried in a wooden ark to a place where the new cycle of the world can begin, the place of the red rocks, Sedona. There are echoes here of the biblical legend of Moses and the bird returning to the Ark with fresh green leaves.

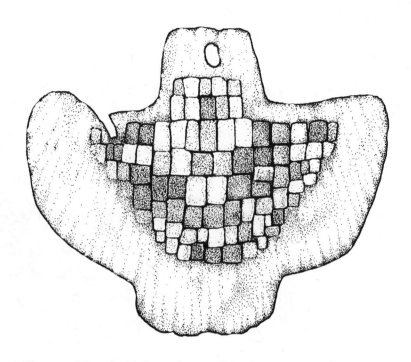

A Sinagua Thunderbird pendant. This shell inlaid with squares of turquoise was found during the excavations of Montezuma Castle.

eagle and macaw feathers are used in Hopi ceremonies today. And, above all, it signifies the consciousness of the land itself, the Ch'i that pulses in the vision of our most expanded moments.

It is therefore fitting that the family of birds be given a place of honor in this geomantic study of Sedona. The Great Bird descends to the southwest in acknowledgement of the places of origin of the Indian peoples. The Great Bird expresses the essence of the geomantic teaching of the Sedona Landscape. And, as the dove descended into Christ and the hawk into the pharaohs, the Great Bird in its graceful movement joins together the worlds of spirit and matter signified by the hexagram and pentagram and opens and activates the chakra system of the temple.

Thus, the bird signifies several things. It is the spirit which mediates between the divine and the human worlds; Christ was filled with the spirit in the form of a descending dove at his baptism. It signifies the transformative principle of life which both impregnates and is given birth to by the Great Mother. It signifies the song of the land and the knowledge of origins. It signifies the mythical remembering of where the people have come from, the reason why parrot, Bird in its graceful movement joins together the worlds of spirit and matter signified by the hexagram and pentagram and opens and activates the chakra system of the temple.

Thus it is appropriate that the rocks be named after birds, especially Horus Rock, the Hawk, who finds his mythological partner in Isis Rock, the topmost point of the hexagram and Thunderbird Rock at the foot of Oak Creek Canyon, the place where the legendary Komwidapokuwia was said to emerge from the hollow log. Geomythically, the telling of the legend of the Great Mother and the Bird brings to life this form of the Sedona Landscape Temple.

As birds take flight and sing their joyful songs, so may we receive from their inspiration the opening to our whole selves, awakening to the consciousness of the earth and of spirit.

Bibliography

Chapter 1

Plateau Magazine of the Museum of Northern Arizona.
    Volume 53. No. 1. *People of the Verde Valley,* 1981.
    Volume 57. No. 1. *Oak Creek Red Rock Country*, 1986.
    Volume 59. No. 4. *The Palatkwapi Trail*, 1987.
Those Who Came Before. R.H. Lister & F.C. Lister. Univ. of Az. Press, 1983.
Anasazi Ruins of the Southwest. W.M. Ferguson & A.H. Rohn. Univ. of N.M., 1987.
Archeological Expeditions to Arizona in 1895. J.W. Fewkes. Bureau of American Ethnology 17th Annual Report, 1895-1896.
The Yavapai of Fort McDowell. Editor Sigrid Khera, 1978.
Violla Jimulla: The Indian Chieftess. Franklin Barnett, 1968.
Arizona As It Was. Hiram Hodge. Rio Grande Press, 1877.
Northeastern and Western Yavapai. E.W. Gifford. University of California Publications in American Archeology and Ethnology.
    Volume 34, 1936.
The Southeastern Yavapai. E.W. Gifford. ibid. Volume 29, 1930-32.
Northeastern and Western Yavapai Myths. E.W. Gifford. Journal of American Folklore. Volume 46, 1933.
University of California Museum of Anthropology: Catalog of Phonograph Cylinders, 1932. Nos. 14-2443 through 14-2454.

Chapter 2

Plateau Volume 53. No. 3. *Water on the Plateau*, 1981.
    Volume 49. No. 1. *Perspectives on the Colorado Plateau*, 1976.
Meteorological/Geological Investigations of the Wupakti Blowhole System.
    J.D. Sartor & D.L. Lamar. Rand Corp, 1962.
Sensitive Chaos. T. Schwenk. New York, Schocken, 1978.
The Fairy Faith in Celtic Countries. J.D. Evans-Wentz, 1911.

Chapter 3

Feng-Shui. E.J. Eitel. Cockaygne, 1973.
Needles of Stone Revisited. T. Graves. Gothic Image, 1986.
Sedona Vortices Update (Cassette). Page Bryant, 1988.

Chapter 4

The Songlines. Bruce Chatwin, 1987.
A Guide to Glastonbury's Temple of the Stars. K.E. Maltwood, 1929.

Chapter 5

Oak Creek Canyon and the Red Rock Country of Arizona. S. Aitchison.
    Still Water Canyon Press, 1978.
The Keltic Power Symbols. N.R. Mann. Triskele, Glastonbury, 1987.
Come Into Animal Presence. (Quoted from *News of the Universe* edited by Robert Bly). Denise Levertov, 1960.

Chapter 6

Sacred Geometry. R. Lawlor. Thames and Hudson, 1982.
Book of the Hopi. F. Waters and Oswald "White Bear" Fredericks. Ballantine Books, 1963.

Chapters 7 & 8

The New View Over Atlantis. John Michell. Thames and Hudson, 1983.
The Dimensions of Paradise. John Michell. Harper and Row, 1988.

Chapters 9 & 10

The Mystical Qabalah. Dion Fortune, 1935.
Song of the Jaguar (Cassette). Anne Williams. Earthsong Productions, 1989.
Four Quartets. T.S. Eliot, 1943.
News of the Universe. Editor Robert Bly. Sierra Club Books, 1980.
Book for the Hours of Prayer. (Quoted from *News of the Universe* edited by Robert Bly). Rainer Maria Rilke, 1899.

Index